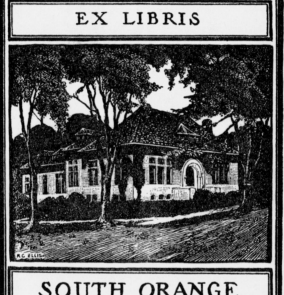

EX LIBRIS

SOUTH ORANGE
PUBLIC LIBRARY

D1384761

KETTI FRINGS

# LOOK
# HOMEWARD,
# ANGEL

A PLAY

*Based on the Novel by* THOMAS WOLFE

WITH AN INTRODUCTION BY EDWARD C. ASWELL

*Charles Scribner's Sons, New York*

## LOOK HOMEWARD, ANGEL

Presented by Kermit Bloomgarden and Theatre 200, Inc., at the Ethel Barrymore Theatre, New York City, November 28th, 1957, with the following cast:

| | |
|---|---|
| BEN GANT | *Arthur Hill* |
| MRS. MARIE "FATTY" PERT | *Florence Sundstrom* |
| HELEN GANT BARTON | *Rosemary Murphy* |
| HUGH BARTON | *Leonard Stone* |
| ELIZA GANT | *Jo Van Fleet* |
| WILL PENTLAND | *Tom Flatley Reynolds* |
| EUGENE GANT | *Anthony Perkins* |
| JAKE CLATT | *Joseph Bernard* |
| MRS. CLATT | *Mary Farrell* |
| FLORRY MANGLE | *Elizabeth Lawrence* |
| MRS. SNOWDEN | *Julia Johnston* |
| MR. FARRELL | *Dwight Marfield* |
| MISS BROWN | *Susan Torrey* |
| LAURA JAMES | *Frances Hyland* |
| W. O. GANT | *Hugh Griffith* |
| DR. McGUIRE | *Victor Kilian* |
| TARKINTON | *Jack Sheehan* |
| MADAME ELIZABETH | *Bibi Osterwald* |
| LUKE GANT | *Arthur Storch* |

DIRECTED BY GEORGE ROY HILL
SETTINGS AND LIGHTING DESIGNED BY JO MIELZINER
COSTUMES BY MOTLEY

# THOMAS WOLFE

## The Playwright Who Discovered He Wasn't

### BY EDWARD C. ASWELL *

THOMAS WOLFE's first great love was the theatre. To see his name in bright lights on Broadway seemed to him, in his youth, the ultimate glory of glories. In pursuit of this ambition, he first studied playwriting under Frederick H. Koch, founder and director of The Carolina Playmakers at the University of North Carolina. There he wrote and acted in several "folk plays," the best known of them being *The Return of Buck Gavin*. In his later years Tom was ashamed of these plays and more than a little scornful of Professor Koch and his concept of folk drama. "We had to write about mountaineers," Tom once told me with a roar of laughter, "whether we had ever seen a mountaineer or not."

After graduating at Chapel Hill, Tom went to Harvard. There for three years he continued to study the art of the dramatist under Professor George Pierce Baker in the famous 47 Workshop. Gradually he began to get an entirely different concept of the function of the artist. As he later stated it to me, with reference to his books: "I have to write about what I know. I cannot write about what I do not know."

Under Baker at Harvard, Tom wrote several plays, the most important being *Mannerhouse* and *Welcome to Our City*. *Mannerhouse* has never been professionally produced except in postwar Germany, where it has had a long run. The theme has to do with the American Civil War and the defeat of a great and gallant people, and their ultimate subjugation by a lesser breed, the rednecks and scalawags who take over after the war and become the new masters. It is easy to see why this theme appeals to the Germans of today.

* Edward C. Aswell, Wolfe's friend and last editor, is now administrator of the Thomas Wolfe Estate.

Judged as a play, *Mannerhouse* can hardly be called successful, for it does not act. It is too full of high-flown talk and murky sentiment. In the maturing of Thomas Wolfe this play is significant chiefly because here, for the first time in his writings, appears a central character named Eugene, who is Thomas Wolfe himself cast backward in time. This Eugene in *Mannerhouse* later became more real and grew into the Eugene of *Look Homeward, Angel*.

*Welcome to Our City* is an altogether different dish of tea. This, his last play under Baker, was an attempt to do the impossible: to portray a whole Southern town, with all its interwoven complexities of character and motive, these complexities eventually working themselves out in racial strife. The town was Altamont, the Altamont of *Look Homeward, Angel*—Tom's birthplace, Asheville. In *Welcome to Our City* there is no Eugene. But add *Mannerhouse* to *Welcome to Our City* and you have the genesis of *Look Homeward, Angel* in Eugene plus Altamont.

*Welcome to Our City* came close to professional production. The Theatre Guild wanted it in 1923, if only Tom would cut it and reduce the large cast of characters. He tried desperately to do this, but each time only succeeded in making the script longer. These frustrating efforts caused Tom to realize at last that perhaps no man ever lived who was less qualified than he to write plays. He could not work within the necessary limitations which the stage imposes. He knew the Guild was right in demanding cuts, but he knew even more surely that he was right in being dissatisfied with the too-long draft the Guild wouldn't take, for in it he had not said half of what he wanted to say, and this is why the play grew longer and longer as he worked to cut it.

When in the end no producer could be found for *Welcome to Our City*, Tom finally came to understand that his trouble lay in trying to employ a literary form to which his talents were not suited. After this, tasting what then seemed the full bitterness of defeat, he began to experiment with a form of writing he had not tried before. It was only in finding out what he was not that he discovered what he was.

At the time he was struggling with his last play, he had said in a letter to Baker: "I have written this play with thirty-odd named characters because it required it, not because I didn't know how to save paint. Some day I'm going to write a play with fifty, eighty, a hundred people—a whole town, a whole race, a whole epoch." Later, this is exactly what he did, but the form in which he did it was not a play—it was a novel called *Look Homeward, Angel*. The town was Altamont. The race was the Gant family (his own family), of whom Eugene was the youngest member. The epoch was the first two decades of this century.

Thomas Wolfe died on September 15, 1938, at the age of thirty-seven. Now, more than nineteen years after his death, *Look Homeward, Angel* has come to Broadway, thanks to the extraordinary insight and dramatic skill of Ketti Frings. How Tom would have rejoiced in this event! It would have been for him the final consummation.

And somehow I cannot think he would have been in the least disturbed by the fact that Ketti Frings has succeeded in doing what he could not do, in adapting for the stage the essence of what he had to say. For, if Tom had lived, he would be content to know that the book as he wrote it is now a great American classic, studied in schools and colleges, published in eleven countries, read by millions; and that it will go on and on as long as there is a younger generation coming up to discover it and to acclaim the young Tom Wolfe as their own most authentic voice.

# CONTENTS

LOOK HOMEWARD, ANGEL

*A Play*

SETTING BY JO MIELZINER

PLACE AND TIME:
THE TOWN OF ALTAMONT, NORTH CAROLINA,
IN THE FALL OF THE YEAR
NINETEEN HUNDRED AND SIXTEEN

# ACT ONE

# ACT ONE

*Scene 1*

*The house is a flimsily constructed frame house of fifteen drafty, various-sized rooms. It has a gabled, unplanned and rambling appearance, and is painted a dirty yellow. Most of its furniture is badly worn and out of style. The beds are chipped enamel-covered iron. There are accordion hat trees, cracked mirrors, an occasional plant. On the typically southern veranda which embraces the front and one side of the house, there are chairs, rockers, and a wood box. There is a sign above the door, electrically lighted at night:* DIXIELAND—ROOMS AND BOARD. *In the center of the house, slightly raised, is a turntable on which all the bedroom scenes are played. At the back of the house a walk approaches the rear of the veranda. There is a side door and near it a circular yard seat. Also down front is a table and a chair.*

*The street itself has a feeling of great trees hanging over it. Occasionally during the play, the stillness is broken by the rustle of autumn leaves, and the poignant wail of a train whistle.*

*The curtain rises in darkness. After a moment we hear* EUGENE's *voice coming from his room. Seated, his back to the audience, he is only partially glimpsed, writing, surrounded by books.*

EUGENE (*Reading*)
"BEN, by Eugene Gant. . . . .
My brother Ben's face is like a piece of slightly yellow ivory . . .

(*Lights come up on the veranda where* BEN GANT, 30, *delicate and sensitive, the most refined of the Gants, and forever a*

19

*stranger among them, is seated on the front steps reading a news-
paper. He is sometimes scowling and surly, but he is the hero
protector of those he loves, with quiet authority and a passion
for home which is fundamental. At times he speaks to the side
over his shoulder, in a peculiar mannerism of speech, as though
he were addressing a familiar unseen presence.*)

EUGENE

His high, white forehead is knotted fiercely by an old man's scowl.
His mouth is like a knife.
His smile the flicker of light across the blade.
His face is like a blade, and a knife, and a flicker of light.
And when he fastens his hard white fingers
And his scowling eyes upon a thing he wants to fix,
He sniffs with sharp and private concentration.

(*Lights reveal* MARIE "FATTY" PERT, 43, *seated near* BEN *in her
rocker. She is a generous, somewhat boozy woman, knitting a pair
of men's socks and tenderly regarding* BEN.)

Thus women looking, feel a well of tenderness
For his pointed, bumpy, always scowling face. . . . ."

(EUGENE *continues writing.*)

BEN

Somebody's got to drive the Huns from the skies. Poor old England
can't be expected to do it alone.

MRS. PERT

It's their mess, isn't it?

BEN

It says here there's an American flying corps forming in Canada.

MRS. PERT

Ben Gant, what are you thinking of?

BEN

All my life in this one little burg, Fatty! Besides getting away, I'd be doing my bit.

MRS. PERT

Would they take you so old?

BEN

This article says eighteen to thirty-two.

MRS. PERT

Aren't the physical standards pretty high?

BEN

Listen to her! I'm in good condition!

MRS. PERT

You're twenty pounds underweight! I never saw anyone like you for not eating.

BEN

Maguire gave me a thorough checkup this spring!

MRS. PERT

How would your family feel, if you went?

BEN

What family? The batty boarders? Apologies, Fatty. I never associate you with them. Except for Gene, nobody'd know I was gone.

(Looks up, dreamily)

To fly up there in the wonderful world of the sky. Up with the angels.

(HELEN GANT BARTON *and her husband* HUGH *enter from the house.* HELEN *is gaunt, raw-boned, in her middle twenties, often nervous, intense, irritable and abusive, though basically generous, the hysteria of excitement constantly lurking in her. It is a spiritual and physical necessity for her to exhaust herself in service to others, though her grievances, especially in her service to her mother, are many.*

HUGH *is a cash register salesman, simple, sweet, extremely warm-hearted. He carries a tray with a coffee pot and cups and saucers which* HELEN *helps him set on a table. They have been arguing.*)

HUGH

We should never have agreed to live here for one day—that's the answer. You work yourself to the bone—for what?

HELEN

Mrs. Pert, the other boarders have almost finished dinner!

MRS. PERT

What's the dessert, Helen?

HELEN

Charlotte Russe.

HUGH

They're like children with a tape worm.

BEN

Fatty, I told you you'd better get in there!

MRS. PERT

I was trying to do without, but I'm afraid that calls me. See you later, Ben.

(*She leaves her knitting on the chair, exits inside.*)

HELEN
Ben, where is Mama?

BEN
How should I know?

HELEN
I've had to serve the entire dinner alone!

HUGH
Look at me, holes in my socks, a trouser button missing—and before I married you I had the reputation of being "dapper."

HELEN
I bet she's off somewhere with Uncle Will, and *I'm* left in the kitchen to slave for a crowd of old cheap boarders! That's her tactic!

HUGH
"Dapper Hugh Barton"—it said so in the newspaper when we were married.

HELEN
(*To* BEN, *who pays no attention*)
You know that, don't you, *don't you?* And do I ever hear her say a word of thanks? Do I get—do I get as much as a go-to-hell for it? No. "Why, pshaw, child," she'll say, "I work more than anybody!" And most time, damn her, she does.

BOARDERS
(*Off stage, calling, ringing the service bell*)
Helen. Helen!

HELEN

You come in, Hugh, and help me!

(HELEN *exits into the house.*)

BEN

How are the cash registers selling, Hugh?

HUGH

Putting the cigar box out of business. I got a good order in Raleigh last week. I've already put away nine hundred dollars toward our own little house.

BEN

You ought to have one, Hugh. You and Helen.

HUGH

(*Looking at part of the newspaper*)

I guess they don't have to advertise the good jobs, do they? The really big jobs . . . . . they wouldn't be here in the newspaper, would they?

BEN

Why?

HUGH

If there was something good here in town . . . not on the road so much . . . . . maybe then I could talk Helen into moving away. Ben, you hear things around the paper—

HELEN

(*Off*)

Hugh! Hugh!

BEN

I'll keep my ears open, Hugh.

HUGH

Well, I guess I don't want to make Helen any madder at me. Thanks, Ben.

(*Exits inside. An automobile is heard off, driving up, stopping.* BEN *moves down to the yard seat, reads his newspaper. The car door slams.*)

ELIZA

(*Off*)

I'll vow I never saw such a man. What little we have got, I've had to fight for tooth and nail, tooth and nail!

(ELIZA GANT *enters with* WILL PENTLAND, *her brother.* ELIZA, 57, *is of Scotch descent, with all the acquisitiveness and fancied premonitions of the Scotch. She is mercurial, with dauntless energy, greed and love. She has an odd way of talking, pursing her lips, and she characteristically uses her right hand in a point-making gesture, fist enclosed, forefinger extended. These mannerisms are often imitated by those who hate and love her.* ELIZA *is carrying some fall leaves and a real estate circular.* WILL *is punchy, successful, secure, a real estate broker. They do not notice* BEN.)

ELIZA

Like the fellow says, there's no fool like an old fool! Of course Mr. Gant's been a fool all his life. Pshaw! If I hadn't kept after him all these years we wouldn't have a stick to call our own.

WILL

You had to have an *artistic* husband.

ELIZA

Artistic. I have my opinion about that. Why, Will, the money that man squanders every year on liquor alone would buy all kinds of good downtown property, to say nothing of paying off this place. We could be well-to-do people now if we'd started at the very beginning.

WILL

You've given him every opportunity.

ELIZA

He's always hated the idea of owning anything—couldn't bear it, he told me once—'cause of some bad trade he made when he was a young man up in Pennsylvania. If I'd been in the picture then, you can bet your bottom dollar there'd been no loss.

WILL

(*Chuckling*)

Or the loss'd been on the other side.

ELIZA

That's a *good* one! You know us Pentlands! Well, I'm going to get after Mr. Gant right today about that bank offer.

WILL

Let me know when you've warmed him up enough for me to talk to him.

ELIZA

It'll take a good deal of warming up, I can tell you. He's so blamed stubborn about that precious old marble yard, but I'll do it!

WILL

Give me a jingle when you want to look at that farm property. I'll drive you out there.

ELIZA

Thanks, Will! I appreciate it.

(WILL *exits.* ELIZA *starts into the house, sees* BEN.)

Ben! What are you doing home at this hour?

BEN

I'm working afternoons this week.

ELIZA

Oh.

(*Somewhat worriedly*)

Will you get dinner downtown?

BEN

I usually do.

ELIZA

You always sound so short with me, Ben. Why is that? You don't even look at me. You know I can't stand not being looked at by the person I'm talking to. Don't you feel well?

BEN

I feel good.

(A *train whistle is heard in the distance.*)

ELIZA

Oh, Pshaw, there's the midday train now! Has Eugene gone to the station?

BEN

How should I know?

ELIZA

(*Calling up to* EUGENE'S *room*)

Eugene, are you up in your room? Eugene?

(EUGENE GANT, *hearing his mother's voice, rises from his chair, turns toward the window, but he doesn't answer, and* ELIZA *does not see him.* EUGENE *is* 17, *the youngest of the* GANTS, *tall, awkward, with a craving for knowledge and love. During the following he leaves his room.*)

Eugene! I'll vow, that boy. Just when I need him. . . .

(*Notices* MRS. PERT'S *knitting*)

Ben, I hope you haven't been lying around here wasting time with that Mrs. Pert again?

BEN

Listen to her! It's the nicest time I spend.

ELIZA

I tell you what: it doesn't look right, Ben. What must the other boarders think? A woman her age . . . . . a drinking woman . . . . married. Can't you find someone young and pretty and free to be with? I don't understand it. You're the best looking boy I've got.

BEN

(*More pleasantly*)

If it'll make you feel better, Mama, I'll look around.

(*Relieved by the change in his mood,* ELIZA *smiles. She also notices the sprawled newspaper.*)

ELIZA

That's Mr. Clatt's newspaper. You know he's finicky about reading it first. Fold it up before you go.

(*During the above,* EUGENE *is seen coming down the stairs from his room. Now limping slightly, he starts to sneak out the side door, but* ELIZA *spots him.*)

**ELIZA**

Eugene, where are you sneaking to? Come out here.

**EUGENE**

(*Comes out*)

Yes, Mama?

**ELIZA**

The train's just coming in. Now you hurry over to that depot.

**EUGENE**

Today? I did it yesterday.

**ELIZA**

Every day until every room is filled. The advertising cards are on the hall table. Go get them.

(EUGENE, *disgruntled, goes into the entry hall to get the cards from a small stand.* ELIZA *strips some dead leaves off a plant.*)

I declare, seventeen is an impossible age. I don't know why he complains. He hasn't anything else to do. Spending his time up there scribbling, dreaming.

**BEN**

The other boarding houses send their porters to the trains.

**ELIZA**

Never you mind, Ben Gant, you used to do it. It's little enough I've ever asked of you boys.

(*To* EUGENE *as he comes from the hall*)

Have you got the cards?

EUGENE
In my pocket.

ELIZA
(*Holding out her hand*)
Let me see them. Let me see them!

EUGENE
(*Takes cards from pocket, reads*)
"Stay at Dixieland, Altamont's Homiest Boarding House."—It should be homliest.

ELIZA
Eugene!

EUGENE
I hate drumming up trade! It's deceptive and it's begging.

ELIZA
Oh my . . . my! Dreamer Eugene Gant, what do you think the world is all about? We are all . . . . all of us . . . . selling something. Now you get over to the depot right this minute. And for heaven's sake, boy, spruce up, shoulders back! Look like you *are* somebody!

(EUGENE *starts off.*)

And smile! Look pleasant!

(EUGENE *grins, maniacly.*)

**BEN**

(*Suddenly, as he watches* EUGENE *limping*)

Gene! What are you walking like that for?

**EUGENE**

Like what?

**BEN**

(*Rises*)

What are you limping for? My God, those are my shoes you've got on! I threw them out yesterday!

**ELIZA**

They're practically brand new.

**BEN**

They're too small for *me*, they must be killing him.

**EUGENE**

Ben, please!

**ELIZA**

Maybe you can afford to throw out brand new shoes.

**BEN**

Mama, for God's sake, you ask him to walk straight, how can he? His toes must be like pretzels!

**EUGENE**

They're all right. I'll get used to them.

**BEN**

(*Throwing down his paper*)

My God, it's a damned disgrace, sending him out on the streets like a hired man . . . Gene should be *on* that train, going to college!

ELIZA

That's enough—that's just enough of that! You haven't a family to provide for like I have, Ben Gant. Now I don't want to hear another word about it! Gene will go to college when we can afford it. This year he can help his Papa at the shop.

BEN

I thought you were going to *warm up* Papa, so he'll sell the shop.

ELIZA

Ben Gant, that wasn't intended for your ears. I'd appreciate it if you wouldn't mention it to Mr. Gant until I have. Hurry off now, son, get us a customer!

EUGENE

Why should Papa sell his shop?

ELIZA

Now you're too young to worry about my business. You tend to yours.

EUGENE

What business do I have to attend to, Mama?

ELIZA

Well, get busy, get busy! Help your Papa at the shop.

EUGENE

I don't want to be a stonecutter.

ELIZA

Well, go back to delivering newspapers. Work for Uncle Will in his real estate office. But keep the ball rolling, child. Now hurry on or you'll be late!

(EUGENE *exits.*)

HELEN

(*Entering*)

Mama, dinner's practically over! I'm no slave!

ELIZA

I'll be right in, Helen.

(HELEN *exits, slamming door.* ELIZA *sighs. For a moment, left alone with* BEN, *she becomes herself, a deeply troubled woman.*)

What's the matter with him, Ben? What's wrong with that boy? What's the matter with all of you? I certainly don't know. I tell you what, sometimes I get frightened. Seems as if every one of you's at the end of something, dissatisfied, and wants something else. But it just can't be. A house divided against itself cannot stand. I'll vow, I don't know what we're all coming to.

(*Approaches side door, pauses*)

If you like, this once, as long as you're home, why don't you eat here? I'm sure there's plenty left over.

BEN

No, thank you, Mama.

(*He starts off.*)

ELIZA

A good hot meal!

BEN

I've got to get over there.

ELIZA

Ben, are you sure you feel all right?

BEN

I feel fine.

ELIZA

Well, have a nice day at the paper, son.

(BEN *exits.* ELIZA *looks after him, then hearing the voices of the boarders, exits into the house by the side door. The boarders, ushered by* HELEN, *enter through the front door. They are:*

JAKE CLATT, 30, *an insensitive boor;*

MRS. CLATT, 60, *Jake's mother, with a coarse smile and dyed hair. She is deaf and carries a cane;*

FLORRY MANGLE, 29, *wistful, humorless, interested in Jake;*

MRS. SNOWDEN, 50, *quiet, unobtrusive, lonely;*

MISS BROWN, 36, *prim on the surface, but with the marks of the amateur prostitute;*

MR. FARREL, 60, *a retired dancing master, new to* DIXIELAND.)

MRS. CLATT

I ate too much again.

HELEN

(*Loudly to* MRS. CLATT)

Help yourself to coffee, please, Mrs. Clatt. I'm short-handed today.

MRS. CLATT

(*Brandishing her cane at* MR. FARREL, *who is about to sit*)

Not there, that's my chair! That one's free, since the school teacher left.

MISS BROWN

You're a teacher too, aren't you, Mr. Farrel?

MR. FARREL

Of the dance. Retired.

MISS BROWN

I hope you'll stay with us for a while. Where are you from?

MR. FARREL

Tampa.

MISS BROWN

Do you know the Castle Walk, Mr. Farrel? I'd love to learn it!

(*They stroll down to the yard seat.*)

MRS. CLATT

I don't know what Mrs. Gant makes this coffee of. There isn't a bean invented tastes like this.

JAKE

Couldn't you make it for us sometime, Helen?

HELEN

My mother always makes the coffee here.

(HUGH *and* MRS. PERT *enter. The others seat themselves.*)

MRS. PERT

That was scrumptious dessert, but oh dear!

(*Sits in her rocker*)

JAKE

Yes, it was good, if only the servings were bigger.

MRS. CLATT

I'm told the best boarding house food in town is down the street at Mrs. Haskells'.

JAKE

That's right, mother. That's what I heard.

HUGH

Then move in to Mrs. Haskells'!

HELEN

(*With a shove*)

Hugh!

(*She exits.*)

MISS MANGLE

I spent one season there, but I prefer it here. It's more informal and entertaining.

JAKE

Not lately. It's been over a month since Mrs. Gant had to have Mr. Molasses Edwards and his two Dixie Ramblers evicted for not paying their rent. She certainly loves to see the police swarm around!

(LAURA JAMES, 23, *carrying a suitcase and a* DIXIELAND *advertising card, enters. She is attractive, but not beautiful. She advances to the steps.*)

MISS MANGLE
Don't you?

JAKE
I like excitement—why shouldn't I?

MISS MANGLE
Other people's excitement. Don't you ever want excitement of your own? I do.

(MRS. CLATT *sees* LAURA, *nudges her son into attention.*)

LAURA
Good afternoon!

HUGH
(*Crosses to her*)
Good afternoon!

LAURA
Is the proprietor here?

HUGH
I'll call her.
(*Calls inside*)
Mrs. Gant! Customer!
(*To* LAURA)
Please come right up.

JAKE
(*Leaping to* LAURA)
Here, let me take that suitcase. It must be heavy for you.

LAURA

Thank you.

(JAKE *takes* LAURA's *suitcase. The other boarders look her over, whisper.* ELIZA, *wearing an apron, places the leaves in a vase on the hall table, enters. At first raking glance she doubts that* LAURA, *so young and different, is a true prospect.*)

ELIZA

Yes?

LAURA

Are you the proprietor?

ELIZA

Mrs. Eliza Gant—that's right.

LAURA

I found this card on the sidewalk.

ELIZA

(*Takes card*)

On the sidewalk! And you're looking for a room?

LAURA

If you have one for me.

ELIZA

Of course I have, dear—a nice quiet room. You just sit down here and have yourself a cup of my *good* coffee, while I go and open it up, so I can show it to you. Hugh, you take care of the young lady. This is Mr. Barton, my son-in-law.

LAURA

How do you do, Mr. Barton? I'm Laura James.

ELIZA

Laura—why that's a *good* Scotch name. Are you Scotch?

LAURA

On one side.

ELIZA

Pshaw! I could have told you were Scotch the minute I laid eyes on you. I'm Scotch too. Well, isn't that nice?

(*Makes introductions*)

Miss James, Mr. Clatt. . . . . .

(*Each acknowledges the introduction according to his personality.*)

. . . . his mother, Mrs. Clatt, Mrs. Snowden, Miss Mangle, Mr. Farrel,

(*Disapprovingly notices* MISS BROWN *with* MR. FARREL.)

. . . . Miss Brown . . . . . *Miss Brown!* And Mrs. Pert. Where do you come from, dear?

LAURA

I live in Richmond.

(MISS BROWN *and* MR. FARREL *exit, practicing the Castle Walk, eventually reappear at the rear of the veranda.*)

ELIZA

Richmond! Now that's a pleasant city—but hot! Not like it is here, cool and refreshing in these hills. You haven't come to Altamont for a cure, have you dear?

LAURA

I'm healthy, if that's what you mean. But I've been working hard and I need a rest.

(HUGH *approaches with coffee.*)

ELIZA

Here's your coffee.

LAURA

(*Takes coffee*)

Thank you, Mr. Barton. What are your rates, Mrs. Gant?

EUGENE

(*Off*)

Mama! Mama!

(EUGENE *runs up the back walk, around the veranda.*)

ELIZA

Suppose I show you the room first.

EUGENE

Mama!

ELIZA

I declare, that child either crawls like a snail or speeds like a fire engine. . . . .

EUGENE

(*Pulls* ELIZA *away from the others*)

Can I speak to you, Mama?

ELIZA

I don't see you limping *now*, when you're not trying to get sympathy. Don't think I don't know your little tricks to. . . .

EUGENE

(*Urgently*)

Mama, Papa's been at Laughran's again. Doctor Maguire is trying to steer him home now.

ELIZA

(*Momentarily stabbed*)

The doctor? Is he sick or is he drunk?

EUGENE

He's rip roaring! He's awful. He kicked Uncle Will again!

(*From offstage come the sounds of a small riot approaching. The occasional bull yell of* GANT, *children chanting "Old Man Gant came home drunk," a dog barking etc.*)

ELIZA

(*Weakly*)

I don't think I can stand it again. A *new* young lady, too.

(EUGENE *turns to see* LAURA, *who, with the other boarders, has heard the approaching* GANT.)

Oh Eugene, why do they keep bringing him home? Take him to a state institution, throw him in the gutter, I don't care. I don't know what to do any more. What'll I do, child?

EUGENE

At least it's been a month this time.

GANT
(*Off*)
Mountain Grills! Stay away from me!

JAKE CLATT
My God, Mr. Gant's on the loose again!

MISS MANGLE
Oh dear, oh dear—

MRS. CLATT
What? What is it?

JAKE CLATT
(*Shouting*)
The old boy's on the loose again!

EUGENE
(*Crossing up to the boarders*)
Would you go inside, all of you, please?

MRS. CLATT
I haven't finished my coffee.

EUGENE
You can wait in the parlor. Please, just until we get him upstairs!

JAKE CLATT
And miss the show?

MISS BROWN
Come along, Mr. Farrel. Let's clear the deck for the old geezer.

MR. FARREL
Perhaps there is some way I can help?


MISS BROWN
I wouldn't recommend it, Mr. Farrel.


JAKE CLATT
Look at him, he's really got a snootful this time!

(EUGENE *urges several of the boarders inside, where they cram in the hallway,* JAKE *and* MRS. CLATT *remain on the porch.* LAURA, *not knowing where to go, remains with* HUGH *outside.*)


GANT
(*Bellowing, off*)
Mountain Grills! Mountain Grills! Fiends, not friends! Don't push me! *Get away from me!*


DOCTOR MAGUIRE
(*Off*)
All right then, Gant, if you can walk, walk!

(ELIZA *stands downstage, stiff and straight.* W. O. GANT, 60, *clatters up the back steps, his arms flailing, his powerful frame staggering, reeling. At heart he is a far wanderer and a minstrel, but he has degraded his life with libertinism and drink. In him still, though, there is a monstrous fumbling for life. He is accompanied by* DR. MAGUIRE, *unkempt but kind, and by* TARKINGTON, *a disreputable crony, also drunk but navigating, and by* WILL PENTLAND.)


DR. MAGUIRE
Here we are, Gant, let's go in the back way.

(GANT *pushes the doctor aside, plunges headlong along the veranda, scattering rockers, flower pots, etc.*)

GANT

Where are you? Where are you? The lowest of the low—boarding house swine! Merciful God, what a travesty! That it should come to this!

EUGENE

Papa, come on. Papa, please!

(EUGENE *tries to take* GANT *by the arm;* GANT *flings him aside.*)

GANT

(*With a sweeping gesture*)

"Waken lords and ladies gay
On the mountain dawns the day—"
Don't let me disturb your little tete-a-tete. Go right ahead, help yourself!

(MRS. CLATT *screams and dashes into the hall.*)

Another helping of mashed potatoes, Mrs. Clatt? Put another tire around your middle—

(EUGENE *tries to catch his father's flailing arms, is flung into* MRS. PERT's *rocker.*)

ELIZA

Mr. Gant, I'd be ashamed. I'd be ashamed.

GANT

Who speaks?

ELIZA

I thought you were sick.

GANT

I am not sick, madame, I am in a wild, blind fury.

(*Raises a chair aloft, threatening* ELIZA. EUGENE *and the* DOCTOR *grab it away from him.*)

ELIZA
Dr. Maguire, get him in the house.

DR. MAGUIRE
Come on, Gant, let me help you.

GANT
(*Plunging down the steps*)
Just one moment! You don't think I know my own home when I see it? This is not where I live. I reside at 92 *Woodson Street.*

DR. MAGUIRE
That was some years ago. This is your home now, Gant.

GANT
This barn? This damnable, this awful, this murderous and bloody barn—home! Holy hell, what a travesty on nature!

WILL
Why don't we carry him in?

DR. MAGUIRE
You keep out of this, Pentland. You're the one who enrages him.

GANT
Pentland—now that's a name for you!
(*Pivots, searching for him*)
Where are you, Will Pentland?
(*Sees him, staggers toward him*)

You're a Mountain Grill! Your father was a Mountain Grill and a horse thief, and he was hanged in the public square.

(*While* HUGH *holds* GANT, EUGENE *brings a cup of coffee.*)

EUGENE
Papa, wouldn't you like some coffee? There's some right here.

GANT
Hah! Some of Mrs. Gant's *good* coffee?

(*He kicks at the coffee cup.*)

Ahh! I'll take some of that *good* bourbon, if you have it, son.

DR. MAGUIRE
Get him a drink! Maybe he'll pass out.

GANT
Drink!

(EUGENE *starts into the house.*)

ELIZA
Gene! Dr. Maguire, you know there isn't a drop of alcohol in this house!

LAURA
I have some.

(*As all stare at her,* LAURA *quickly opens her handbag, takes from it a small vial, crosses to the doctor.*)

I always carry it in case of a train accident.

GANT
Well, what are we waiting for, let's have it!

DR. MAGUIRE

(*Taking the vial*)

Good God, this won't fill one of his teeth.

GANT

(*Roars*)

Well, let's have it!

(LAURA *backs away in fear.* HELEN *enters, the joy of being needed shining on her face.*)

DR. MAGUIRE

You can have it, Gant, but you'll have to come up onto the veranda to drink it—

GANT

Mountain Grills! Vipers! Lowest of the low! I'll stand here until you take me home. *Isn't anybody going to take me home?*

HELEN

Papa! Why have you been drinking again when you know what it does to you?

GANT

(*Weakens, leans against her*)

Helen—I have a pain right here.

HELEN

Of course you do. Come with me now. I'll put you to bed, and bring you some soup.

(HELEN *takes the huge man's arm, leads him toward the veranda.* HELEN's *success with* GANT *etches itself deeply into* ELIZA's *face.*)

GANT

Got to sit down—

(*Sits on edge of veranda*)

Sit down, Helen, you and me. Sit and talk. Would you like to hear some Keats . . . . . beautiful Keats?

ELIZA

(*Crossing up to veranda, angrily*)

He's got his audience now. That's all he wants.

EUGENE

Mama, he's sick!

ELIZA

Mr. Gant, if you feel so bad, why don't you act nice and go inside? The whole neighborhood's watching you.

GANT

(*Wildly sings*)

"Old Man Gant came home drunk. . . . .

(TARKINGTON *joins him.*)

Old Man Gant came home drunk. . . . . ."

TARKINGTON

(*Singing, waving his arms*)

"Old Man Gant came home. . . . ."

(*His joy fades as he sees* ELIZA *glaring at him.*)

ELIZA

Were you drinking with him too, Mr. Tarkington?

TARKINGTON
Sev-everal of us were, Mrs. Gant, I regret to say.

ELIZA
(*Pulling* TARKINGTON *to his feet*)
I'll have Tim Laughran thrown in jail for this.

TARKINGTON
He started out so peaceable like. . . . .

ELIZA
(*Pushing him toward rear exit of veranda*)
I've warned him for the last time.

TARKINGTON
Just on beer!

ELIZA
*Get off my premises!*

(TARKINGTON *exits.* GANT *groans.*)

HELEN
Dr. Maguire's here to give you something for your pain, Papa.

GANT
Doctors! Thieves and bloodsuckers! "The paths of glory lead but to
the grave."—Gray's Elegy. Only four cents a letter on any tombstone
you choose, by the master carver! Any orders?

(*Groans, weak with pain*)

It's the devil's own pitchfork. Don't let them put me under the
knife—promise me, daughter. Promise me!

(HELEN *nods. With a giant effort,* GANT *pulls himself up.*)

GANT

"Over the stones, rattle his bones! He's only a beggar that nobody owns."

MAGUIRE

Good God, he's on his feet again!

EUGENE

Hugh, let's get him in the house.

GANT

(*Throwing off* HUGH *and* EUGENE)

I see it! I see it! Do you see the Dark Man's shadow? There! There he stands—the Grim Reaper—as I always knew he would. So you've come at last to take the old man home? Jesus, have mercy on my soul!

(GANT *falls to the ground. There is an agonized silence.* EUGENE, THE DOCTOR, *and* HUGH *rush to him.*)

ELIZA

(*Anxiously*)

Dr. Maguire?

(DR. MAGUIRE *feels* GANT's *heart.*)

DR. MAGUIRE

He's just passed out, Mrs. Gant. Men, let's carry him up!

(HUGH, WILL, MAGUIRE *and* EUGENE, *lift the heavy body, quickly carry* GANT *inside.* HELEN *follows.* ELIZA, *saddened and miserable, starts to gather up the coffee cups.* LAURA *picks up her suitcase and starts off.* ELIZA *turns, sees her.*)

ELIZA

Oh, Miss James. I was going to show you that room, wasn't I?

(*Siezes* LAURA's *suitcase*)

LAURA

Hmmmmm?

ELIZA

I think you'll enjoy it here. It's quiet and peaceful—oh, nobody pays any mind to Mr. Gant. I'll tell you what; we don't have occurrences like this every day.

LAURA

Well, how much is it?

ELIZA

Twenty—fifteen dollars a week. Three meals a day, and the use of electricity and the bath. Do you want me to show it to you?

LAURA

No, I'm sure it will be all right.

ELIZA

(*Starting in, turns back*)

That's in advance, that is.

(LAURA *opens her purse, takes out a roll of one dollar bills, puts them one by one into* ELIZA's *outstretched hand.*)

LAURA

One, two, three—I always keep my money in one dollar bills—it feels like it's more.

ELIZA
(*Almost cheerful again*)
Oh, I know what you mean.

(MR. FARREL *enters by the side door with his suitcase. He is hoping to sneak out.*)

ELIZA
(*Sees him as the paying business continues*)
Mr. Farrel! Where are you going? Mr. Farrel, you've paid for a week in advance!

(MR. FARREL *wordlessly gestures that it's all too much for him, exits.*)

ELIZA
Well, they come and they go. And you're here now, isn't that nice?

LAURA
. . . Nine . . . . ten. . . .

(BEN *enters from the other direction, hurriedly.*)

BEN
I heard about father—how is he?

ELIZA
Drunk. Dr. Maguire's taking care of him now. Ben, this is Miss James . . . . this is my son, Ben Gant.

BEN
(*Impressed by her looks, nods*)
Miss James.

LAURA

(*Barely looking at* BEN, *nods*)

—fourteen, fifteen. There.


ELIZA

(*Puts the money in bosom of her dress*)

Thank you dear. Miss James is going to stay with us a while, we hope! I'll take you up, dear. You'll be cozy and comfortable here.

(*They start inside.*)

I'll show you the rest of the house later.


LAURA

(*Turning in doorway*)

Nice to have met you, Mr. Gant.

(ELIZA *and* LAURA *exit.*)


BEN

(*Imitating* LAURA's *disinterest, as he picks up cup of coffee*)

Nice to have met you, Mr. Gant.

(*Shrugs, drinks coffee.* WILL *enters from the house, still sweating.*)


WILL

That father of yours. Do you know he kicked me? I don't want to tell you where. Why don't you watch out for him more, Ben? It's up to you boys, for your mother's sake—for Dixieland. I warned her about him . . . . a born wanderer like he is, and a widower. But you can't advise women—not when it comes to love and sex.

(*He starts off, stops.*)

You might thank me for my help. No one else has.

BEN
Thank you, Uncle Will.

WILL
Bunch of ungrateful Gants. You're the only one of them who has any class.

(WILL *exits.* BEN *lights a cigarette.* EUGENE *enters.*)

EUGENE
Did you hear about it, Ben?

BEN
There isn't a soul in town who hasn't.

EUGENE
What's it all about? It doesn't make sense. Can you figure it out, Ben? Why does he do it?

BEN
How should I know?

(*Drinks his coffee*)

Is Maguire almost through?

EUGENE
(*Hurt, not understanding* BEN's *preoccupation*)

Ben, remember in the morning when we used to walk together and you were teaching me the paper route? We talked a lot then.

BEN
Listen to him! We're talking.

EUGENE
If he hates it so much here, why does he stay?

BEN

You stupid little fool, it's like being caught in a photograph. Your face is there, and no matter how hard you try, how are you going to step out of a photograph?

(DOCTOR MAGUIRE *enters.*)

Shut up now, will you. Hello, Doc.

DR. MAGUIRE

Your sister sure can handle that old goat like a lamb! The funny thing though is that people like him. He's a good man, when sober.

BEN

Is he all right?

DR. MAGUIRE

He's going to be.

BEN

Can I speak to you a minute about me? If you have a minute.

DR. MAGUIRE

Shoot, Ben.

BEN

(*To* EUGENE)

Haven't you got something else to do?

EUGENE

(*Seating himself*)

No.

DR. MAGUIRE

What's the matter—you got pyorrhea of the toenails, or is it something more private?

BEN

I'm tired of pushing daisies here. I want to push them somewhere else.

DR. MAGUIRE

What's that supposed to mean?

BEN

I suppose you've heard there's a war going on in Europe? I've decided to enlist in Canada.

EUGENE
(*Rises*)

What do you want to do that for?

BEN
(*To* EUGENE)

You keep out of this.

DR. MAGUIRE

It is a good question, Ben. Do you want to save the world? This world?

BEN

In Christ's name, Maguire, you'll recommend me, won't you? You examined me just a couple of months ago.

DR. MAGUIRE
(*Puts down his bag*)

Well, let's see, for a war the requirements are somewhat different. Stick out your chest.

(BEN *does so;* THE DOCTOR *looks him over.*)

Feet? Good arch, but pigeon-toed.


BEN
Since when do you need toes to shoot a gun?


DR. MAGUIRE
How're your teeth, son?


BEN
Aren't you overdoing it, Doc?

(BEN *draws back his lips and shows two rows of hard white grinders. Unexpectedly,* MAGUIRE *prods* BEN's *solar plexis with a strong yellow finger and* BEN's *distended chest collapses. He sinks to the veranda edge, coughing.*)


EUGENE
What did you do that for?


DR. MAGUIRE
They'll have to save this world without you, Ben.


BEN
(*Rises, grabs* THE DOCTOR)
What do you mean?


DR. MAGUIRE
That's all. That's all.


BEN
You're saying I'm not all right?


DR. MAGUIRE
Who said you weren't all right?

BEN

Quit your kidding.

DR. MAGUIRE

What's the rush? We may get into this war ourselves before too long. Wait a bit.

(*To* EUGENE)

Isn't that right, son?

BEN

I want to know. Am I all right or not?

DR. MAGUIRE

Yes, Ben, you're all right. Why, you're one of the most all right people I know.

(*Carefully, as he feels* BEN's *arms*)

You're a little run down, that's all. You need some meat on those bones.

(BEN *breaks from him, moves away.*)

You can't exist with a cup of coffee in one hand and a cigarette in the other. Besides, the Altamont air is good for you. Stick around. Big breaths, Ben, big breaths.

(*Picks up his bag*)

BEN

Thanks. As a doctor, you're a fine first baseman.

DR. MAGUIRE

Take it easy. Try not to care too much.

(*Exits*)

EUGENE

He's right. You should try to look after yourself more, Ben.

(EUGENE *tries to comfort* BEN. BEN *avoids his touch, lurches away.*)

BEN

He doesn't have any spirit about this war, that's all that's the matter with him.

(BEN *recovers his coffee, drinks.* EUGENE *studies him.*)

EUGENE

I didn't know you wanted to get away from here so badly.

BEN

(*Looks over at* EUGENE, *puts down coffee*)

Come here, you little bum.

(EUGENE *approaches close.*)

My God, haven't you got a clean shirt?

(*He gets out some money.*)

Here, take this and go get that damn long hair cut off, and get some shoes that fit, for God's sake. You look like a lousy tramp. . . .

EUGENE

(*Backing away*)

Ben, I can't keep taking money from you.

BEN

What else have you got me for?

(*The brothers roughhouse playfully with the money,* EUGENE *giggling. Then, with sudden intense ferocity,* BEN *seizes* EUGENE's *arms, shakes him.*)

You listen to me. Listen to me. You go to college, understand? Don't settle for anyone or anything—learn your lesson from me! I'm a hack on a hick paper—I'll never be anything else. You can be. Get money out of them, anyway you can! Beg it, take it, steal it, but get it from them somehow. Get it and get away from them. To hell with them all!

(BEN *coughs.* EUGENE *tries to help him.* BEN *escapes, sits tiredly on the veranda's edge.* EUGENE *disconsolately sinks into a nearby chair.*)

Neither Luke, nor Stevie, nor I made it. But you can, Gene. I let her hold on and hold on until it was too late. Don't let that happen to you. And Gene, don't try to please everyone—please yourself.

(BEN *studies* EUGENE, *realizes his confusion and depression. Then, noticing* LAURA's *hat which she has left on the yard table, he points to it.*)

Where's she from?

EUGENE

(*Follows* BEN's *gaze to* LAURA's *hat, picks it up, sniffs it*)

I don't know. I don't even know her name.

BEN

Miss James. I'll have to announce her arrival in my society column.

(*Takes hat from* EUGENE, *admires it*)

The firm young line of spring . . . . budding, tender, virginal. "Like something swift, with wings, which hovers in a wood—among the feathery trees, suspected, but uncaught, unseen." Exquisite.

(*Returns hat to table, rises*)

Want to walk downtown with me? I'll buy you a cup of mocha.


EUGENE

Maybe I ought to stay here.


BEN

(*Ruffling* EUGENE's *hair*)

With her around I don't blame you. I dream of elegant women myself, all the time.


EUGENE

(*Rising*)

You do? But, Ben, if you dream of elegant women, how is it . . . well—


BEN

Mrs. Pert? Fatty's a happy woman—there's no pain in her she feels she has to unload onto someone else. Besides, she's as adorable as a duck. Don't you think so?


EUGENE

I guess you're right. I like her—myself . . . sure.


BEN

Someday you'll find out what it means. I've got to get back to work.


EUGENE

Ben, I'm glad they won't take you in Canada.

BEN

(*With that upward glance*)

Listen to him! I was crazy to think of going. I have to bring you up first, don't I?

(BEN *exits.* EUGENE *walks about restlessly, looks up at* LAURA'S *window.* MISS BROWN, *dressed for a stroll, carrying a parasol, enters from the house.*)

MISS BROWN

Gene! You haven't even said hello to me today.

EUGENE

Hello, Miss Brown.

MISS BROWN

My, everything's quiet again. Lovely warm day, isn't it?

(MISS BROWN *sings and dances sensuously for* EUGENE.)

"Pony boy, pony boy,
Won't you be my pony boy?
Don't say no, can't we go
Right across the plains?

(MISS BROWN *approaches* EUGENE; *he backs away from her, stumbling against the table.*)

Marry me, carry me
Far away with you!

(*She starts out through rear veranda.*)

Giddy-ap, giddy-ap, giddy-ap. Oh!
My pony boy!"

(MISS BROWN *exits.* EUGENE *sits on the yard seat, takes off one shoe and rubs his aching toes.* LAURA *enters, picks up her hat, sees* EUGENE. EUGENE *hides his shoeless foot.*)

MISS BROWN
(*Off stage, fainter*)
"Pony boy, pony boy
Mmmm, mmm, mmmm—Mmmmm, mmmm, mmmm,
Marry me, carry me
Far away with you!
Giddy-ap, giddy-ap, giddy-ap. Oh!
My pony boy."

(*At the door,* LAURA *looks again at* EUGENE, *smiles, exits.*)

### CURTAIN

# ACT ONE

*Scene 2*

*The night is sensuous, warm. A light storm is threatening. Long, swaying tree shadows project themselves on the house. Seated on the side veranda are* JAKE, MRS. CLATT, FLORRY, MISS BROWN, *and* MRS. SNOWDEN. MRS. PERT *is seated in her rocker,* BEN *on the steps beside her. They are drinking beer.* MRS. PERT *measures the socks she is knitting against* BEN'S *shoe.* JAKE CLATT *softly plays the ukelele and sings.* EUGENE *is sitting on the side door steps, lonely, yearning.*

JAKE

(*Singing*)

"K-k-katy, K-k-katy" (*etc.*)

(*As* JAKE *finishes,* FLORRY *gently applauds.* JAKE *starts softly strumming something else.*)

MRS. PERT

(*To* BEN, *quietly*)

I know you talked to the doctor today. What did he say? Tell Fatty.

BEN

I'm out before I'm in. Oh, I know you're pleased, but you don't know how it feels to be the weakling. All the other members of this family—they're steers, mountain goats, eagles. Except father, lately —unless he's drunk. Do you know, though, I still think of him as I

64

thought of him as a little boy—a Titan! The house on Woodson Street that he built for Mama with his own hands, the great arm-loads of food he carried home . . . the giant fires he used to build. The women he loved at Madame Elizabeth's. Two and three a night, I heard.

MRS. PERT

It's nice for parents to have their children think of them as they were young.

(As BEN *chuckles*)

I mean, that's the way I'd like my children to think of me. Oh, you know what I mean.

BEN

(*Laughs with his typical glance upward*)

Listen to her!

MRS. PERT

Ben, who are you always talking to, like that?

(*Imitates* BEN *looking up over his shoulder*)

BEN

Who, him?

(*She nods*)

That's Grover, my twin. It was a habit I got into, while he was still alive.

MRS. PERT

I wish you'd known me when I was young. I was some different.

BEN

I bet you weren't half as nice and warm and round as you are now.

MRS. PERT

Ben, don't ever let your mother hear you say those things. What could she think?

BEN

Who cares what she thinks?

MRS. PERT

Dear, I only hope when the right girl comes along you won't be sorry for the affection you've lavished on me.

BEN

I don't want the *right girl*. Like some more beer? I've got another bottle.

MRS. PERT

Love some more, honey.

(BEN *rises, searches under the yard table for the bottle he has hidden, realizes it's not there, suspiciously looks at* EUGENE. EUGENE *innocently gestures, then reaches behind him and tosses the beer bottle to* BEN. BEN *and* FATTY *laugh.* BEN *returns with the beer to* FATTY *as* LAURA *enters from the house.*)

JAKE

(*Rising expectantly*)

Good evening, Miss James.

LAURA

Good evening.

JAKE

Won't you sit down?

MRS. CLATT
(*As* LAURA *seems about to choose a chair*)
That's Mr. Farrel's. Your's is back there!

JAKE
(*Loudly*)
Mr. Farrel has left, Mother.

MRS. CLATT
What?

JAKE
Never mind.
(*To* LAURA)
No sense in being formal. Won't you sing with me, Miss James?

LAURA
I love music, but I have no talent for it.
(LAURA *moves toward rear of veranda, away from the others.*)

FLORRY
(*To* JAKE)
I love to sing.
(JAKE *ignores* FLORRY, *follows after* LAURA, FLORRY *tugging at* JAKE'S *coat.*)

MRS. SNOWDEN
(*To* JAKE *as he passes*)
Do you know Indiana Lullaby? It's a lovely song.
(JAKE *and* LAURA *exit.*)

BEN

I'm comfortable when I'm with you, Fatty.

MRS. PERT

That's good, so'm I.

BEN

People don't understand. Jelly roll isn't everything, is it?

MRS. PERT

Ben Gant, what kind of a vulgar phrase is that?

BEN

It's a Stumptown word. I used to deliver papers there. Sometimes those negro women don't have money to pay their bill, so they pay you in jelly roll.

MRS. PERT

Ben—your little brother's right over there listening!

BEN

(*Glances toward* EUGENE)

Gene knows all about jelly roll, don't you? Where do you think he's been all his life—in Mama's front parlor?

EUGENE

Oh, come on, Ben!

BEN

(*Laughs*)

There's another word I remember in the eighth grade. We had a thin, anxious looking teacher. The boys had a poem about her.

(*Quotes*)

"Old Miss Groody
Has good Toody."

FATTY
Ben, stop it!

(*They both laugh.* LAURA *has managed to lose* JAKE, *and has strolled around the back of the house. She enters to* EUGENE *from the side door.*)

LAURA
Good evening.

EUGENE
What!

LAURA
I said good evening.

EUGENE
(*Flustered*)
Goodyado.

LAURA
I beg your pardon?

EUGENE
I mean—I meant to say good evening, how do you do?

LAURA
Goodyado! I like that much better. Goodyado!

(*They shake hands,* LAURA *reacting to* EUGENE'S *giant grip.*)

Don't you think that's funny?

EUGENE

(*Sits on yard seat*)

It's about as funny as most things I do.

LAURA

May I sit down?

EUGENE

(*Leaping up*)

Please.

LAURA

(*As they both sit*)

I'm Laura James.

EUGENE

I know. My name's Eugene Gant.

LAURA

You know, I've seen you before.

EUGENE

Yes, earlier this afternoon.

LAURA

I mean before that. I saw you throw those advertising cards in the gutter.

EUGENE

You did?

LAURA

I was coming from the station. You know where the train crosses the street? You were just standing there staring at it. I walked right by you and smiled at you. I never got such a snub before in my whole life. My, you must be crazy about trains.

EUGENE

You stood right beside me? Where are you from?

LAURA

Richmond, Virginia.

EUGENE

Richmond! That's a big city, isn't it?

LAURA

It's pretty big.

EUGENE

How many people?

LAURA

Oh, about a hundred and twenty thousand, I'd say.

EUGENE

Are there a lot of pretty parks and boulevards?

LAURA

Oh yes . . .

EUGENE

And fine tall buildings, with elevators?

LAURA

Yes, it's quite a metropolis.


EUGENE

Theatres and things like that?


LAURA

A lot of good shows come to Richmond. Are you interested in shows?


EUGENE

You have a big library. Did you know it has over a hundred thousand books in it?


LAURA

No, I didn't know that.


EUGENE

Well, it does. I read that somewhere. It would take a long time to read a hundred thousand books, wouldn't it?


LAURA

Yes, it would.


EUGENE

I figure about twenty years. How many books do they let you take out at one time?


LAURA

I really don't know.


EUGENE

They only let you take out two here!

LAURA

That's too bad.

EUGENE

You have some great colleges in Virginia. Did you know that William and Mary is the second oldest college in the country?

LAURA

Is it? What's the oldest?

EUGENE

Harvard! I'd like to study there! First Chapel Hill. That's our state university. Then Harvard. I'd like to study all over the world, learn all its languages. I love words, don't you?

LAURA

Yes, yes, I do.

EUGENE

Are you laughing at me?

LAURA

Of course not.

EUGENE

You are smiling a lot!

LAURA

I'm smiling because I'm enjoying myself. I like talking to you.

EUGENE

I like talking to you, too. I always talk better with older people.

LAURA

Oh!


EUGENE

They know so much more.


LAURA

Like me?


EUGENE

Yes. You're very interesting.


LAURA

Am I?


EUGENE

Oh yes! You're very interesting!

(JAKE CLATT *approaches,* FLORRY MANGLE *hovering anxiously on the veranda.*)


JAKE CLATT

Miss James?


LAURA

Yes, Mr. Platt?


JAKE CLATT

Clatt.


LAURA

Clatt.

JAKE CLATT
Jake Clatt! It's a lovely evening. Would you like to take a stroll?

LAURA
It feels to me like it's going to rain.

JAKE CLATT
(*Looking at the sky*)
Oh, I don't know.

EUGENE
(*Rising, moving in between* LAURA *and* JAKE)
It's going to rain, all right.

JAKE CLATT
Oh, I wouldn't be so sure!

LAURA
Perhaps some other time, Mr. Clatt.

JAKE CLATT
Certainly. Good night, Miss James. Good night, sonny.

(EUGENE *glares after* JAKE, *who returns to the veranda. The other boarders have disappeared.* JAKE *and* FLORRY *exit.* FATTY *and* BEN *still sit on the steps. A train whistle moans mournfully in the distance.* EUGENE *cocks an ear, listens.*)

LAURA
You *do* like trains, don't you?

EUGENE
Mama took us on one to St. Louis to the Fair, when I was only five. Have you ever touched one?

LAURA
What?

EUGENE
A locomotive. Have you put your hand on one? You have to feel
things to fully understand them.

LAURA
Aren't they rather hot?

EUGENE
Even a cold one, standing in a station yard. You know what you
feel? You feel the shining steel rails under it . . . and the rails send
a message right into your hand—a message of all the mountains that
engine ever passed—all the flowing rivers, the forests, the towns, all
the houses, the people, the washlines flapping in the fresh cool
breeze—the beauty of the people in the way they live and the way
they work—a farmer waving from his field, a kid from the school
yard—the faraway places it roars through at night, places you don't
even know, can hardly imagine. Do you believe it? You feel the
rhythm of a whole life, a whole country clicking through your hand.

LAURA
(*Impressed*)
I'm not sure we all would. I believe *you* do.

(*There is a moment while* LAURA *looks at* EUGENE. BEN *moves
up to the veranda and the phonograph, plays the record "Genevieve."* EUGENE *and* LAURA *speak simultaneously.*)

EUGENE                                    LAURA
How long do you plan to . . .            How old are you . . . ?

EUGENE

I'm sorry—please.

(*Draws a chair close to* LAURA, *straddles it, facing her*)

LAURA

No, you.

EUGENE

How long do you plan to stay here, Miss James?

LAURA

My name is Laura. I wish you'd call me that.

EUGENE

Laura. It's a lovely name. Do you know what it means?

LAURA

No.

EUGENE

I read a book once on the meaning of names. Laura is the laurel. The Greek symbol of victory.

LAURA

Victory. Maybe someday I'll live up to that!

(*After a second*)

What does Eugene mean?

EUGENE

Oh, I forget.

LAURA

You, forget?

EUGENE

It means "well born."


LAURA

How old are you?


EUGENE

Why?


LAURA

I'm always curious about people's ages.


EUGENE

So am I. How old are you?


LAURA

I'm twenty-one. You?


EUGENE

Nineteen. Will you be staying here long?


LAURA

I don't know exactly.


EUGENE

You're only twenty-one?


LAURA

How old did you think I was?


EUGENE

Oh, about that. About twenty-one, I'd say. That's not old at all!

LAURA
(*Laughs*)
I don't feel it is!


EUGENE
I was afraid you might think I was too young for you to waste time
with like this!


LAURA
I don't think nineteen is young at all!


EUGENE
It isn't, really, is it?


LAURA
Gene, if we keep rushing together like this, we're going to have a
collision.

(LAURA *rises, moves away from* EUGENE. *He follows her. They
sit together on the side steps, reaching with whispers toward each
other. The turntable revolves, removing* EUGENE'S *room and re-
vealing* GANT'S *room.*)


FATTY
Ben, what's your full name?


BEN
Benjamin Harrison Gant. Why?


FATTY
I thought Ben was short for benign.


BEN
Benign! Listen to her!

*(They laugh. The lights come up in* GANT's *bedroom.* ELIZA, *carrying a pitcher and a glass, enters.* GANT *is in bed, turned away from her.)*

GANT

Helen?

ELIZA

*(Bitterly)*

No, it's not Helen, Mr. Gant.

*(Pours a glass of water)*

GANT

*(Without turning)*

If that's water, take it away.

ELIZA

Why aren't you asleep? Do you have any pain?

GANT

None but the everyday pain of thinking. You wouldn't know what that is.

ELIZA

I wouldn't know?

*(She starts picking up* GANT's *strewn clothing.)*

GANT

How could you? You're always so busy puttering.

ELIZA

All the work I do around here, and you call it puttering?

GANT

Some people are doers, some are thinkers.


ELIZA

Somebody has to *do*, Mr. Gant. Somebody has to. Oh! I know you look on yourself as some kind of artist fella—but personally, a man who has to be brought maudlin through the streets—screaming curses—if you call that artistic!


GANT

The hell hound is at it again. Shut up, woman!


ELIZA

Mr. Gant, I came in here to see if there was something I could do for you. Only pity in my heart. Now will you please turn over and look at me when I talk to you? You know I can't stand being turned away from!


GANT

You're a bloody monster, you would drink my heart's blood!


ELIZA

You don't mean that—we've come this far together, I guess we can continue to the end. You know I was thinking only this morning about that first day we met. Do you realize it was thirty-one years ago, come July?


GANT

(*Groaning*)

Merciful God, thirty-one long miserable years.


ELIZA

I can remember like it was yesterday. I'd just come down from Cousin Sally's and I passed by your shop and there you were. I'll

vow you looked as big as one of your tombstones—and as dusty—
with a wild and dangerous look in your eye. You were romantic in
those days—like the fellow says, a regular courtin' fool—"Miss Pentland," you said, "you have come into this hot and grubby shop like
a cooling, summer shower—like a cooling, summer shower." That's
just what you said!

GANT

And you've been a wet blanket ever since.

ELIZA

I forgive you your little jokes, Mr. Gant. I forgive your little jokes.

(*Sits beside him, finds needle and thread under her collar, mends
his dressing gown*)

GANT

Do you?

(*Slowly turns and looks at her finally*)

Do you ever forgive me, Eliza? If I could make you understand
something. I was such a strong man. I was dozing just now, dreaming
of the past. The far past. The people and the place I came from.
Those great barns of Pennsylvania. The order, the thrift, the plenty.
It all started out so right, there. There I was a man who set out to
get order and position in life. And what have I come to? Only riot-
ing and confusion, searching and wandering. There was so much
before, so much. Now it's all closing in. My God, Eliza, where has it
all gone? Why am I here, now, at the rag end of my life? The years
are all blotted and blurred—my youth a red waste—I've gotten old,
an old man. But why here? Why here?

ELIZA

You belong here, Mr. Gant, that's why! You belong here.

(*She touches his hand.*)

GANT

(*Throws away her hand*)

And as I get weaker and weaker, you get stronger and stronger!

ELIZA

Pshaw! If you feel that way, it's because you have no position in life. If you'd ever listened to me once, things would have been different. You didn't believe me, did you, when I told you that little, old marble shop of yours would be worth a fortune someday? Will and I happened to be downtown this morning . . .

(GANT *groans*)

. . . and old Mr. Beecham from the bank stopped us on the street and he said, "Mrs. Gant, the bank is looking for a site to build a big new office building, and do you know the one we have our eye on?" And I said, "No." "We have our eye on Mr. Gant's shop, and we're willing to pay twenty thousand dollars for it!" Now, what do you think of that?

GANT

And you came in here with only pity in your heart!

ELIZA

Well, I'll tell you what, twenty thousand dollars is a lot of money! Like the fellow says, "It ain't hay!"

GANT

And my angel, my Carrara angel? You were going to sell her too?

ELIZA

The angel, the angel, the angel. I'm so tired of hearing about that angel!

GANT

You always have been. Money dribbled from your honeyed lips, but never a word about my angel. I've started twenty pieces of marble trying to capture her. But my life's work doesn't interest you.


ELIZA

If you haven't been able to do it in all these years, don't you think your gift as a stonecutter may be limited?


GANT

Yes, Mrs. Gant, it may be limited. It may be limited.


ELIZA

Then why don't you sell the shop? We can pay off the mortgage at Dixieland and then just set back big as you please and live off the income from the boarders the rest of our lives!


GANT

(*Furious, he all but leaps from the bed.*)

Oh holy hell! Wow-ee! The boarders! That parade of incognito pimps and prostitutes, calling themselves penniless dancing masters, pining widows, part-time teachers and God knows what all! Woman, have mercy! That shop is my last refuge on earth. I beg you—let me die in peace! You won't have long to wait. You can do what you please with it after I've gone. But give me a little comfort now. *And leave me my work!* At least my first wife understood what it meant to me.

(*He sentimentally seeks the plump pillow.*)

Cynthia, Cynthia . . .


ELIZA

(*Coldly*)

You promised me you would never mention her name to me again.

(*There is a long silence.* ELIZA *bites the sewing thread.*)

Mr. Gant, I guess I never will understand you. I guess that's just the way it is. Good night. Try to get some sleep.

(*She rises, tucks the bed clothes about him.*)

I reckon it's like the fellow says, some people never get to understand each other—not in this life.

(ELIZA *exits, stands outside* GANT's *door, trying to pull herself together.*)

GANT
(*Moans*)

Oh-h-h, I curse the day I was given life by that blood-thirsty monster up above. Oh-h-h, Jesus! I beg of you. I know I've been bad. Forgive me. Have mercy and pity upon me. Give me another chance in Jesus' name. . . . Oh-h-h!

(*The turntable removes* GANT's *room, replacing it with* EUGENE's *room. Lights come up on the veranda.* LAURA *and* EUGENE *still sit on the side steps.* FATTY *and* BEN, *as earlier, seated, are softly laughing.* ELIZA, *bitterly warped by her scene with* GANT, *enters. She starts gathering up the boarders' coffee cups and saucers.*)

MRS. PERT
(*A little giddy*)

Why, if it isn't Mrs. Gant! Why don't you sit down and join us for awhile?

ELIZA
(*Her sweeping glance takes in the beer glasses.*)

I've told you before, Mrs. Pert, I don't tolerate drinking at Dixieland!

BEN
Oh, Mama, for God's sake . . .

ELIZA

(*Angrily turns off the phonograph*)

You two can be heard all over the house with your carrying on.

BEN

Carrying on—listen to her!

ELIZA

You're keeping the boarders awake.

BEN

They just went in!

ELIZA

As I came past your door just now, Mrs. Pert, there was a light under it. If you're going to spend all night out here, there's no sense in wasting electricity.

BEN

The Lord said "Let there be light," even if it's only 40 watts.

ELIZA

Don't you get on your high horse with me, Ben Gant. You're not the one who has to pay the bills! If you did, you'd laugh out of the other side of your mouth. I don't like any such talk. You've squandered every penny you've ever earned because you've never known the value of a dollar!

BEN

The value of a dollar!

(*Rises, goes into hall to get his jacket*)

Oh, what the hell's the use of it anyway? Come on, Fatty, let's go for a stroll.

FATTY

(*Rises*)

Whatever you say, Ben, old Fatty's willing.


ELIZA

(*Attacking* MRS. PERT)

I don't want any butt-ins from you, do you understand? You're just a paying boarder here. That's all. You're not a member of my family, and never will be, no matter what low methods you try!


EUGENE

(*Leaving* LAURA, *miserable*)

Mama, please!


ELIZA

(*To* EUGENE)

I'm only trying to keep decency and order here, and this is the thanks I get! You should all get down on your knees and be grateful to me!


BEN

(*Coming out of hall, slamming the screen door*)

What am I supposed to be grateful for? For what?


FATTY

(*Trying to stop it*)

Ben, Ben, come on.


BEN

For selling the house that papa built with his own hands and moving us into this drafty barn where we share our roof, our food, our pleasures, our privacy so that you can be Queen Bee? Is that what I'm supposed to be grateful for?

ELIZA

(*Picks up bottle and glasses*)

It's that vile liquor that's talking!


EUGENE

Let's stop it! For God's sake, let's stop it! Mama, go to bed, please. Ben . . .

(EUGENE *sees that* LAURA *has exited into the house. He frantically looks after her.*)


BEN

Look at your kid there! You've had him out on the streets since he was eight years old—collecting bottles, selling papers—anything that would bring in a penny.


ELIZA

Gene is old enough to earn his keep!


BEN

Then he's old enough for you to let go of him! But no, you'd rather hang on to him like a piece of property! Maybe he'll grow in value, you can turn a quick trade on him, make a profit on him. He isn't a son, he's an investment! You're so penny-mad that—

(*Shifting the bottles and glasses into one hand,* ELIZA *slaps* BEN. *There is a long silence. They stare at each other.*)


BEN

Come on, Fatty.

(BEN *exits, past* FATTY, *down the street.*)


FATTY

He didn't mean it, Mrs. Gant.

(*She follows* BEN.)

Ben? Ben, wait for Fatty!

(A *moment's pause*)

EUGENE
(*Quietly, miserably*)
Mama. Mama. Mama!

ELIZA
Well, she puts him up to it! He never used to talk to me like that.
You stood right there and saw it. Now I'll just ask you: was it my
fault? Well, was it?

EUGENE
(*Looks after* LAURA)
Mama, Mama, in God's name go to bed, won't you? Just go to bed
and forget about it, won't you?

ELIZA
All of you. Every single one of you. Your father, then Ben, now
you . . . you all blame me. And not one of you has any idea, any
idea . . you don't know what I've had to put up with all these years.

EUGENE
Oh Mama, stop! Please stop!

ELIZA
(*Sinking onto the steps*)
I've done the best I could. I've done the best I could. Your father's
never given me a moment's peace. Nobody knows what I've been
through with him. Nobody knows, child, nobody knows.

EUGENE

(*Sits beside her*)

I know, Mama. I do know. Forget about it! It's all right.


ELIZA

You just can't realize. You don't know what a day like this does to me. Ben and I used to be so close—especially after little Grover died. I don't think a mother and son were ever closer. You don't remember when he was a youngster, the little notes he was always writing me. I'd find them slipped under my door, when he got up early to go on his paper route . . . "Good morning, Mama!" . . . "Have a nice day, Mama . ." We were so close . . .


EUGENE

It's late. You're tired.


ELIZA

(*Managing to pull herself together, rises*)

Well, like the fellow says, it's no use crying over *that* spilt milk. I have all those napkins and towels to iron for tomorrow.


EUGENE

(*Rises, looking toward* LAURA's *room*)

The boarders can get along without new napkins tomorrow, Mama. Why don't you get some sleep?


ELIZA

Well, I tell you what: I'm not going to spend my life slaving away here for a bunch of boarders. They needn't think it. I'm going to sit back and take things as easy as any of them. One of these days you may just find us Gants living in a big house in Doak Park. I've got the lot—the best lot out there. I made the trade with old Mr. Doak himself the other day. What about that?

(*She laughs.*)

He said, "Mrs. Gant, I can't trust any of my agents with you. If I'm to make anything on this deal, I've got to look out. You're the sharpest trader in this town!" "Why, pshaw, Mr. Doak," I said (I never let on I believed him or anything), "all I want is a fair return on my investment. I believe in everyone making his profit and giving the other fellow a chance. Keep the ball a-rolling," I said, laughing as big as you please!

(*She laughs again in recollection.*)

"You're the sharpest trader in this town." That's exactly his words. Oh, dear.

(EUGENE *joins her laughter.*)

Well . . . I'd better get at those napkins. Are you coming in, child?

EUGENE
(*Looks toward* LAURA's *room*)
In a little while.

ELIZA
Don't forget to turn off the sign. Goodnight, son.

(EUGENE *returns to* ELIZA. *She kisses him.*)

Get a *good* night's sleep, boy. You mustn't neglect your health.

(*She starts in.*)

EUGENE
Don't work too late.

(EUGENE *starts toward the side door.*)

ELIZA

Gene, you know where Sunset Terrace runs up the hill? At the top of the rise? Right above Dick Webster's place. That's my lot. You know where I mean, don't you?

EUGENE

Yes, Mama.

ELIZA

And that's where we'll build—right on the very top. I tell you what, though, in another five years that lot'll bring twice the value. You mark my words!

EUGENE

Yes, Mama. Now, for God's sake, go and finish your work so you can get to sleep!

ELIZA

No sir, they needn't think I'm going to slave away all my life. I've got plans, same as the next fellow! You'll see.

(*Off stage, the church chimes start to sound the midnight hour.*)

Well, good night, son.

EUGENE

Good night, Mama . .

(ELIZA *exits.* EUGENE *calls with desperate softness.*)

Laura . . . Laura!!

(*Gives up, turns away.* LAURA *enters through the side door.* EUGENE *turns, sees her.*)

Did you hear all that? I'm sorry, Laura.

LAURA

What's there to be sorry about?

EUGENE
Would you like to take a walk?

LAURA
It's a lovely evening.

EUGENE
It might rain.

LAURA
I love the rain.

(EUGENE *and* LAURA *hold out their hands to each other.* EUGENE *approaches her, takes her hand. They go off together. For a moment the stage is silent.* ELIZA *enters with an envelope in her hand.*)

ELIZA
See, looky here—I made a map of it. Sunset Terrace goes . .

(*She looks around.*)

Gene? Eugene?

(*She looks up towards* EUGENE'S *room.*)

Gene, I asked you to turn out the sign! That boy. I don't know what I'm going to do with him.

(ELIZA *goes into the hall, turns out the sign and stands for a moment. Offstage, a passerby is whistling "Genevieve."* ELIZA *comes down to the edge of the veranda and looks out into the night in the direction taken by* BEN *and* FATTY.)

Ben? Ben?

SLOW CURTAIN

ACT TWO

# ACT TWO

*Scene 1*

GANT'S MARBLE YARD AND SHOP

*A week later.*

*Under a high, wide shed is the sign:* W. O. GANT—STONE CARVER. *The shed is on a back street, behind the town square. In the distance can be seen the outline of Dixieland. Inside the shed are slabs of marble and granite and some finished monuments . . . . an urn, a couchant lamb and several angels. The largest and most prominent monument is a delicately carved angel of a lustrous white Carrara marble, with an especially beautiful smiling countenance. There is a cutting area down stage right, protected from the sun by a shade, where* EUGENE, *wearing one of his father's aprons, is discovered operating a pedalled emery wheel. At the other side of the shed is an office with a grimy desk, a telephone, and a curtain into another room beyond. A sidewalk runs between the shed and a picket fence up stage. Near the office is a stone seat, bearing the inscription, "Rest here in peace."*

ELIZA *enters from the street. The prim shabbiness of her dress is in contrast to her energetic mood and walk.*

ELIZA
(*Crosses to office, calls inside*)
Mr. Gant! Mr. Gant!

EUGENE
(*Stops wheel, calls*)
Papa's not here now, Mama.

97

ELIZA

(*Approaches* EUGENE *just as he accidently blows some marble dust in her face*)

Where is he? Gene, you know I can't stand that marble dust—will you step out here where I can talk to you?

(*As* EUGENE *ambles out to her*)

Besides, I can't stand not to see the face I'm talking to. My goodness, spruce up, boy—how many times do I have to tell you? Shoulders back—like you *are* somebody. And smile, look pleasant.

(EUGENE *gives that idiotic grin.*)

Oh pshaw! I hope your father's not over at you-know-where again.

EUGENE

He went to buy a newspaper for the obituaries.

ELIZA

How enterprising of him! But he won't follow up on it. Oh no, he says it's ghoulish to contact the bereaved ones right off. I declare, tombstones are no business anyway, anymore—in this day and age people die too slowly.

(*Sinks onto stone seat, leans back, for a brief instant seems actually to rest*)

I tell you what, this feels good. I wish I had as much time as some folks and could sit outside and enjoy the air.

(*Observes* EUGENE, *looking at her dress as he works lettering a marble slab*)

What are you looking at? I don't have a rent, do I?

EUGENE

I was just noticing you have on your dealing and bargaining costume again.

ELIZA

Eugene Gant, whatever do you mean by that? Don't I look all right? Heaven knows, I always try to look neatly respectable.

EUGENE

Come on, Mama.

ELIZA

What! I declare! I might have a better dress than this, but law's sake, there's some places it don't pay to advertise it! Oh, Gene, you're smart, smart, I tell you! You've got a future ahead of you, child.

EUGENE

Mama, what kind of a future have I got if I can't get an education?

ELIZA

Pshaw, boy, you'll get your education if my plans work out! I'll tell you what though—in the meantime, it wouldn't hurt you to work in Uncle Will's office, would it?

EUGENE

I don't know anything about real estate, Mama.

ELIZA

What do you have to know? Buying and selling is an instinct, and you've got it. You've got my eye for looking and seeing and remembering, and that's what's important. Why, there isn't a vital statistic about a soul in Altamont I don't carry right in my head. What they make, what they owe—what they're hiding, what they show!

(*She laughs, enjoying her cleverness.*)

You see, Eugene, I'm a poet, too—"a poet and I don't know it, but my feet show it—they're longfellows!"

(*She leans back, chuckles.*)

Oh dear, I can't get a smile out of you this morning. You've been so strange all this last week.

(*Rises, slaps him on the back*)

Gene, stand with your shoulders back. If you go humped over, you'll get lung trouble sure as you're born.

(*Moves upstage, looks toward the town center where she presumes* GANT *is*)

That's one thing about your papa: he always carried himself straight as a rod. Of course, he's not as straight now as he used to be—Gene, *what* in the world are you standing on one foot and then the other for? Do you have to go to the bathroom?

EUGENE

Mama! Asking me that at my age!

ELIZA

Then why are you fidgeting? It's not often we have a nice chance to chat like this.

EUGENE

Papa's paying me thirty cents an hour!

ELIZA

Paying you? How did you manage that?

EUGENE

I told him I needed the money.

ELIZA

For heaven's sake, what for? You've got your room and board.

EUGENE

Don't you think I need new clothes for one thing?

ELIZA

Pshaw! The way you're still growing? It doesn't pay.

(*She purses her lips, looks at him significantly.*)

Has my baby gone and got himself a girl?

EUGENE

What of it? What if it were true? Haven't I as much right as anyone?

ELIZA

Pshaw! You're too young to think of girls, especially that Miss James. She's practically a mature woman compared to you. I don't think you realize how young you are, just because you're tall and read a lot of books.

(*Sound of car.* ELIZA *looks off.*)

Pshaw! That's your Uncle Will come for me. Say, how long does it take your father to buy a newspaper, anyway?

EUGENE

He said he'd be right back. Is it something important?

ELIZA

Oh, I've got plans, Gene, plans for him, plans for all of us. Well, tell him I'll be back. Second thought, don't tell him, I'll just catch him. I want you to be here too. Work hard, child!

(ELIZA *exits, the car leaves.* EUGENE *approaches the Carrara angel, touches the draped folds over her breast.* GANT *enters, watches, smiling. He has had a few beers, but he is not drunk.* EUGENE *becomes aware of his father's presence, starts guiltily.*)

GANT

I've done that myself many a time, son. Many a time. Well, what did your mother have to say?

EUGENE

Did you see her?

GANT

I've been sitting over at Laughran's waiting for her to leave. What a longwinded bag!

EUGENE

You promised the doctor you wouldn't go to Laughran's.

GANT

(*Putting on his apron*)

What difference does it make? A couple of beers won't hurt what I've got. Was that Will Pentland she went off with?

EUGENE

Yes.

GANT

Aha! And she said she'd be back?

EUGENE

Yes.

GANT

I have a mind what she's up to. She'll be back with freshly drawn up papers tucked in her bosom. Yes, when you touch the breast of Miss Eliza, you feel the sharp crackle of bills of sale, not like the bosom of this angel. She begins to look better after a bath, doesn't she? I've been neglecting her lately. My, how she gleams!

EUGENE

(*Sits below angel*)

Papa, you were young when you got married, weren't you?

GANT

What?

EUGENE

When did you get married?

GANT

It was thirty-one bitter years ago when your mother first came wriggling around that corner at me like a snake on her belly. . . .

EUGENE

I don't mean Mama. How old were you when you were first married? To Cynthia?

GANT

By God, you better not let your mother hear you say that name!

EUGENE

I want to know . . . . how old were you?

GANT

Well, I must have been twenty-eight. Ah, Cynthia, Cynthia.

EUGENE

You loved her, didn't you, Papa?

GANT

She had a real glowing beauty. Sweet, noble, proud, and yet soft, soft—she died in her bloom.

EUGENE

She was older than you, wasn't she?

GANT

Yes. Ten years.

EUGENE

Ten years! But it didn't make any difference, did it?

GANT

(*Confidingly*)

She was a skinny, mean, tubercular old hag who nearly drove me out of my mind!

EUGENE

(*Shocked*)

Then why do you talk about her the way you do? To Mama?

GANT

Because I'm a bastard, Gene. I'm a bastard!

(LAURA *enters, carrying a picnic basket, her mood somewhat restless.*)

Say, isn't this a pretty little somebody looking for you?

EUGENE

Laura!

LAURA

Hello, Mr. Gant.

GANT

Hello!

LAURA

Hello, Gene. So this is your shop!

GANT

This is a real pleasure. It's not often I see *smiling* people around here. Haven't you got fed up with our little resort, young lady?

LAURA

I'm really just beginning to enjoy it here.

GANT

What do you find to enjoy about it?

LAURA

Oh, the countryside is beautiful. Gene and I have had lots of pleasant walks in the hills.

GANT

Oh, so it's Gene who makes it pleasant for you, hey?

EUGENE

(*Taking off his apron*)

Papa!

GANT

You're fond of Gene, aren't you?

LAURA

He's very nice and intelligent.

GANT

Gene's a good boy—our best.

LAURA

(*Looking around*)

My, isn't this place interesting? How did you happen to become a stonecutter, Mr. Gant?

(EUGENE *studies* LAURA *during this, sensing her evasiveness.*)

GANT

Well, I guess you'd call it a passion with some people. When I was a boy Gene's age, I happened to pass a shop something like this.

(*Of the angel*)

And this very angel was there. She's Carrara marble, from Italy. And as I looked at her smiling face, I felt, more than anything in the world, I wanted to carve delicately with a chisel. It was as though, if I could do that, I could bring something of me out onto a piece of marble. Oh, the reminiscences of the old always bore the young.

LAURA

No, they don't.

GANT

So I walked into that shop, and asked the stonecutter if I could become an apprentice. Well, I worked there for five years. When I left, I bought the angel.

(*He looks at the angel with longing.*)

I've hardly had her out of my sight since. I bet I've started twenty pieces of marble, but I've never been able to capture her. . . . . I guess there's no use trying anymore. . . .

(*He becomes silent, morose. Sensitively,* EUGENE *touches his father's shoulder, looks at* LAURA).

EUGENE

Would you like to look around, Laura?

LAURA

I'm afraid I'm bothering you at your work.

GANT

(*Looks at* EUGENE, *coming out of his distant thought and mood*)

No, no. Show her about, Gene.

(*Suddenly, decisive*)

I have some other things I must do . . .

(*Starts toward office, pauses*)

—though some people find looking at tombstones depressing. Still, we all come to them in the end.

(GANT *exits.*)

EUGENE

Why do you think you might be bothering me?

LAURA

You are supposed to be working.

EUGENE

You came here to see me. What's happened, Laura? Something's different today.

LAURA

Oh, don't pay any attention to me. I just . . . . I don't know.

EUGENE

What's in the basket?

LAURA

I asked Helen to pack us a picnic lunch.

EUGENE

Good! Let's go!

LAURA

(*Puts basket on marble slab*)

Not now.

EUGENE

(*Puts his arm around her*)

What is it, Laura? What's the matter? Have I done something wrong?

LAURA

(*Shakes her head*)

Gene, Helen knows about us! And your father too.

EUGENE

I don't care—I want the whole world to know.

(*Picks up basket*)

Here, let's go.

LAURA

No. Let's not talk about it.

(*Sits on stool, near slab*)

This is pretty marble. Where's it from?

EUGENE

Laura, you don't give a damn where that marble came from!

LAURA

(*Starts to cry*)

Oh, Gene, I'm so ashamed, so ashamed.

EUGENE

(*Sits beside her on slab*)

Laura, my darling, what is it?

LAURA

Gene, I lied to you—I'm twenty-three years old.

EUGENE

Is that all?

LAURA

You're not nineteen either. You're seventeen.

EUGENE

I'm a thousand years old, all the love I've stored up for you.

(*Again puts his arms around her*)

LAURA

(*Struggling away*)

I'm an older woman. . . .

EUGENE

In God's name, what does that have to do with us?

LAURA

There have to be rules!

EUGENE

Rules are made by jealous people. They make rules to love by so
even those with no talent for it can at least pretend. We don't need
rules. We don't have to pretend. Oh, Laura, my sweet, what we have
is so beautiful, so rare . . . . how often in life can you find it?

LAURA

(*Escaping his arms, rises*)

Eugene, you're a young boy, a whole world just waiting for you.

EUGENE

You are my world, Laura. You always will be. Don't let anything destroy us. Don't leave me alone. I've always been alone.

LAURA

It's what you want, dear. It's what you'll always want. You couldn't stand anything else. You'd get so tired of me. You'll forget—you'll forget.

EUGENE

I'll never forget. I won't live long enough.

(*Takes her in his arms, kisses her*)

Will you forget?

LAURA

(*As he holds her*)

Oh my darling, every word, every touch, how could I?

EUGENE

Then nothing has changed. Has it? Has it?

MADAME ELIZABETH'S VOICE

(*Off*)

Good morning!

(MADAME ELIZABETH, 38, *the town madame, enters along the street. She is well clad, carries herself stylishly. She sees* EUGENE *and* LAURA, *stops.* EUGENE *and* LAURA *break from each other.*)

**EUGENE**
Good morning, Madame Elizabeth.

**MADAME ELIZABETH**
Is Mr. Gant here?

**EUGENE**
He's inside.

**MADAME ELIZABETH**
Well, don't let me keep you from what you're doing.

(*Approaches office, calls*)

Mr. Gant!

(LAURA *and* EUGENE *exit into yard.* GANT, *changed into a better pair of trousers, tying his tie, enters.*)

**GANT**
Elizabeth, my dear Elizabeth! Well, this is a surprise!

(*Seizes her hands*)

**MADAME ELIZABETH**
(*Sentimentally looking him over*)

Six years, W.O. Six years—except to nod to. Time, what a thief you are.

**GANT**
He hasn't stolen from you—you're still as handsome and stylish as ever. Won't you sit down?

**MADAME ELIZABETH**
Oh, W.O.—you and your gallant manners. But I'm no chicken any-

more, and no one knows it better than I do. If you only knew how often we talk about you up on Eagle Crescent. What a man you were! Wild! Bacchus himself. You remember the song you used to sing?

GANT

Life was many songs in those days, Elizabeth.

MADAME ELIZABETH

But when you got liquored up enough—don't you remember? Of course I can't boom it out like you do.

(*Sings, imitating* GANT. GANT *joins her.*)

"Up in that back room, boys,
Up in *that* back room,
All those kisses and those hugs,
Among the fleas and bugs.
In the evening's gloom, boys,
I pity your sad doom.
Up in that back room, boys,
Up in *that* back room."

(*They both laugh.* GANT *gives her an affectionate fanny slap.*)

GANT

The loss of all that—that's the worst, Elizabeth.

MADAME ELIZABETH
(*Sitting on the bench*)

Oh, W.O., W.O.! We do miss you.

GANT
(*Joining her on the bench*)

How are all the girls, Elizabeth?

MADAME ELIZABETH

(*Suddenly distressed*)

That's what I came to see you about. I lost one of them last night.

(*Takes handkerchief from her pocket, quietly cries into it*)

GANT

Oh. I'm sorry to hear that.

MADAME ELIZABETH

Sick only three days. I'd have done anything in the world for her. A doctor and two trained nurses by her all the time.

GANT

Too bad. Too bad. Which one was it?

MADAME ELIZABETH

Since your time, W.O. We called her Lily.

GANT

Tch . . . tch . . . tch. Lily.

MADAME ELIZABETH

I couldn't have loved her more if she had been my own daughter. Twenty-two, a child, a mere child. And not a relative who would do anything for her. Her mother died when she was thirteen, and her father is a mean old bastard who wouldn't even come to her death-bed.

GANT

He will be punished.

MADAME ELIZABETH

As sure as there's a God in heaven—the old bastard! I hope he rots! Such a fine girl, such a bright future for her. She had more opportunities than I ever had—and you know what I've done here. I'm a rich woman today, W.O. Why, not even your wife owns more property than I do. I beg your pardon—I hope you don't mind my speaking of her—

(GANT *gestures to go right ahead.*)

Mrs. Gant and I both understand that property is what makes a person hold one's head up! And Lily could have had all that too. Poor Lily! No one knows how much I'll miss her.

(*A moment's quiet.* GANT *is respecting her grief.*)

GANT
I suppose you'll be wanting something for her grave?

(*As* MADAME ELIZABETH *nods, he rises.*)

Here's a sweet lamb . . . . *couchant* lamb, it's called. *Couchant* means lying-down in French. That should be appropriate.

MADAME ELIZABETH
No, I've already made up my mind. . . .

(*Rises, moves toward the Carrara angel*)

I want that angel.

GANT
You don't want *her*, Elizabeth. Why, she's a white elephant. Nobody can afford to buy her!

MADAME ELIZABETH
I can and I want her.

GANT
My dear Elizabeth, I have other fine angels. What about this one? My own carving.

MADAME ELIZABETH

No. Ever since I first saw that angel, I thought, when somebody who means something to me goes, she's going to be on the grave.

GANT

That angel's not for sale, Elizabeth.

MADAME ELIZABETH

Then why should you have her out here?

GANT

The truth is, I've promised her to someone.

MADAME ELIZABETH

I'll buy her from whoever you promised and give them a profit. Cash on the line. Who did you sell it to?

GANT

My dear Madame Elizabeth. Here is a nice expensive Egyptian urn. Your beloved Lily would like that.

MADAME ELIZABETH

Egyptian urns—pah! Pea pots! I want the angel!

GANT

(With growing intensity)

It's not for sale! Anything you like . . . . . everything you like . . . . I'll give it to you. . . . . I'll make you a present, for old times' sake. But not my angel!

MADAME ELIZABETH

Now let's not waste any more time over this. How much, W.O.?

GANT

She's Carrara marble from Italy, and too good for any whore!

(*He calls.*)

Eugene . . . . . . Eugene!

MADAME ELIZABETH
(*Furious*)

Why you old libertine, how dare you speak to me like that?

EUGENE
(*Entering, with* LAURA)

What is it, father? What's the matter?

MADAME ELIZABETH

Your father's a stubborn old nut, that's what!

GANT
(*Crosses toward office, turns*)

I'm sorry if I've offended you.

MADAME ELIZABETH

You have, W.O., deeply!

GANT

Gene, will you be so kind and see if you can wait upon the Madame?

(*Exits into the inner room of the office*)

MADAME ELIZABETH

I've heard the trouble your mother has with the old terror—now I believe it! All I'm asking is that he sells me that angel—for one of my dear girls who's gone—a dear, young girl in the flower of her life . .

(*Of* LAURA)

. . . . . like this young girl here.

EUGENE

Madame Elizabeth, I believe Papa is saving that angel for his own grave.

MADAME ELIZABETH

(*Sits on bench*)

Oh-h-h, why didn't he say so? Why didn't he tell me? Poor, poor W.O. Well, of course in that case. . . . .

(*She partially recovers. To* LAURA)

If you were to think of *your* death, dear—if you can, I mean, and we never know, we never know—is there something here that would appeal to you?

LAURA

(*Looks around*)

I like the little lamb.

MADAME ELIZABETH

Lambs are for children, aren't they?

EUGENE

(*Stoops behind lamb*)

Lambs are for anybody. Put your hand on it. Feel it.

(*He takes* MADAME ELIZABETH'S *hand, strokes it across the lamb.*)

Isn't it cool and content and restful? And you could have a poem engraved on the base.

MADAME ELIZABETH

A poem. . . .

EUGENE

Let's see if we can find something you'd like.

(*Picks up book*)

Here's a book of Fifty Fine Memorial Poems.

(MADAME ELIZABETH *still strokes the lamb.* EUGENE *finds a poem.*)

See if you like this. . . .

(*Reads*)

"She went away in beauty's flower,
Before her youth was spent;
Ere life and love had lived their hour,
God called her and she went."

(MADAME ELIZABETH *sobs.*)

"Yet whispers faith upon the wind;
No grief to her was given.
She left your love and went to find
A greater one in heaven."

MADAME ELIZABETH

(*Quoting, through her heartfelt tears*)

"She left *your* love and went to find
A greater one in heaven. . . ."

(*Rises, addresses* EUGENE)

I hope you never lose someone you love, boy. Well, let me know when the little lying-down lamb is ready.

(*She nods with majestic dignity to* LAURA, *exits.* WILL *and* ELIZA *enter, look off in the direction taken by* MADAME ELIZABETH.)

ELIZA

Don't stare after her, Will! You know who that is.

(To EUGENE)

Was that shameless woman here to see your father?

EUGENE

One of the girls at Eagle Crescent died. She bought a monument.

ELIZA

Oh she did! She bought one! Well, your father certainly has to deal with all kinds of people. Will, go in and tell Mr. Gant that we're here.

(WILL *exits.* ELIZA *looks at* LAURA.)

Oh, Miss James! It's five minutes to dinner time at Dixieland, and you know the rules about being late.

EUGENE

(*Crosses to pick up basket*)

Laura and I are going on a picnic.

ELIZA

Not now you're not.

(To LAURA)

My dear, I want to talk privately to Mr. Gant—to Eugene, too, and I've asked Ben to join us.

EUGENE

We've made plans, Mama.

ELIZA

Son, this is a family conference.

LAURA

Gene, please—I'll wait for you over at Woodruff's. Please.

(LAURA *and* EUGENE *stroll off, whispering.* WILL *enters from office, paring his nails.*)

ELIZA

Is he in there?

WILL

He's there. We've got him cornered.

(*They chuckle.* BEN, *looking feverish and ill, enters.*)

BEN

Hello, Uncle Will. Hello, Mama—you look like you just swallowed fifty or a hundred acres. What did you buy today?

ELIZA

Now, Ben, it just happens that today we're selling—I hope we are anyway.

BEN

What's it all about?

ELIZA

You just sit down there. I may not need you, but I want you to be here.

BEN

(*Sits beneath the angel*)

I hope it won't take long.

(GANT *enters. He wears a coat of carefully brushed black wool, a tie, and carries his hat which he leaves just inside the office.*)

GANT

Good morning, Miss Eliza.


ELIZA

My, how elegant! Aren't we burning a river this morning?


GANT

I heard you were out here, Miss Eliza. I so seldom have a visit from
you!

(*He gestures the tribute.*)


ELIZA

That's most gracious. You may all sit down now. Gene! Will!

(EUGENE *enters, sits.* WILL *sits on office step.* GANT *moves a chair
center.*)

Now, Mr. Gant. . . .


GANT

(*As he sits*)

This isn't one of your temperance meetings?


ELIZA

(*A bit surprised*)

Our private temperance problem—that's a part of it, yes. Mr. Gant,
how old are you?


GANT

I've lost track.


ELIZA

You're sixty years old in December. And if Dr. Maguire were here,
he could tell you . . .

GANT

I've heard what Doc Maguire has to tell me. I shouldn't be lifting these marbles. I shouldn't be drinking liquor. I should take a nice, long rest.

ELIZA

Then you save me a great deal of argument about that. Now, Gene . . .

EUGENE

Yes, Mama?

ELIZA

You want to go to college, don't you?

EUGENE

Very much.

ELIZA

Well, I figure that four years at Chapel Hill will cost thirty-four hundred dollars—but of course you'll have to wait on tables. Otherwise it would be forty-four hundred dollars, which is ridiculous—at the moment we don't even have thirty-four hundred dollars.

GANT

Oh, for God's sake, get to the point, Miss Eliza. Have you got the papers from the bank?

ELIZA

(*Stands in front of him*)

Why, what do you mean, what papers?

GANT

You know what I mean. Fish for them, woman!

(*Pointing to her bosom*)

*Go ahead, fish for them.*

(ELIZA *turns her back, from her bosom fishes out a large envelope.* GANT *laughs, a roaring bitter laugh, leaps up to* EUGENE, *who joins the laughter.*)

ELIZA

(*Angrily*)

What in the world are you two hyenas laughing at?

GANT

Oh, as you would say, Miss Eliza, that's a good one, that's a *good* one.

ELIZA

Well, I am glad to see you in a *good mood.*

GANT

So the bank wants this little old lot, here? That's what you told me, didn't you? Though I can't for the life of me see why?

WILL

There's a new business street going through here in a few months.

GANT

Let me see the check.

ELIZA

(*Takes check from envelope, hands it to him*)

Well, it's for twenty thousand dollars. Will had to guarantee it personally for me to bring it here. Did you ever see anything like it. Two–zero–comma–zero–zero–zero–decimal–zero–zero!

GANT

W. O. Gant. It seems to be in good order all right.

ELIZA

Well, it is—and Will's looked over this deed, and it's all in order too, isn't it, Will?

(*Hands the deed to* GANT)

Give me your pen, Will.

WILL

(*Hands* ELIZA *the pen*)

And I just had it filled.

GANT

(*Examining the deed*)

This fine print . . . . . I really do need glasses.

ELIZA

(*Puts pen on work table*)

You can trust Will. He's been all over it, Mr. Gant!

GANT

(*Looks at angel*)

What about the marble stock and the monuments?

ELIZA

They're not included.

EUGENE

Papa—the years you've spent here . . . . all your fine work. Please don't give it up!

ELIZA

Now, Gene, your father knows what he's doing.

EUGENE

But he's such a fine stonecutter!

GANT

You think my work is fine, son?

EUGENE

Isn't it, Ben?

(GANT *crosses down right into the marble yard, looking about.*)

ELIZA

Your father knows his duty to all of us—and to himself.

EUGENE

There isn't a cemetery in the state that isn't filled with his work— you can always recognize it. Clean, and pure, and beautiful. Why should he give it up?

ELIZA

Why, law, I don't say he should give it up entirely. He can have another little shop further out of town!

EUGENE

But he's too old to transplant now, Mama. This is his street. Everyone knows him here. People pass by. Mr. Jannadeau's shop next door, and Woodruff's across the way—all the people and places Papa knows!

GANT

And Tim Laughran's down the block!

ELIZA

(*Crosses down to* GANT)

Oh, yes. That's another reason for getting rid of this place. Put yourself out of temptation's way, Mr. Gant.

GANT

(*Sits on slab*)

I certainly do love it here.

EUGENE

Don't give it up, Papa!

BEN

What do you want to do to him, Mama?

ELIZA

Now looky here—you are a fine stonecutter—why, haven't I always said so? But it's time you rested. You want to live a long time, don't you?

(*Sits beside him on slab*)

GANT

Well, sometimes I'm not sure.

ELIZA

Well, you do—and I want you to live a long time—we all want to! People can talk about a short but sweet life, but we all want to live! Look at me, I'm fifty-seven years old. I've borne nine children, raised six of them, and worked hard all my life. I'd like to back up and rest a little myself. And we can, Mr. Gant. If you'll just sign that little slip of paper. I guarantee, in a year from now, you'll have completely forgotten this dingy, crooked, dusty yard. Won't he, Ben? Won't he? Ben!

**BEN**

Some people have trouble forgetting some things, Mama.

**ELIZA**

Why pshaw, I'm going to *see* to it that he forgets it. I'll have time to look after you. Won't I, Mr. Gant?

**GANT**

You're right about one thing, Miss Eliza, that I can't dispute. You have worked hard.

(*Rises, moves to center work table*)

**EUGENE**

Papa, please, don't do it.

(GANT *sits at work table, signs the deed.* ELIZA *crosses to him, picks it up.*)

**ELIZA**

Thank you, Mr. Gant. Now the check. You know what I'm going to do? I'm going to plan a great, glorious celebration.

(*Gives the deed to* WILL, *speaks to* EUGENE)

We'll ask your brother Luke to come home, if the Navy will let him out. And we'll invite Stevie, and Daisy and her husband, too, except if she brings those whiny children of hers.

(*Notices* GANT *just looking at the check*)

Turn it over, Mr. Gant. Sign it on the back.

GANT

Why do I have to sign it?


ELIZA

Endorse it, that's all. W. O. Gant, like it's written on the front of the check.


GANT

That can wait until I offer it, can't it?


ELIZA

To clear the check, Mr. Gant!


GANT

I'm not used to these things. How do you clear it?


ELIZA

You sign it—I'll deposit it in the Dixieland account, then we draw checks on it.


GANT

We?


ELIZA

Yes. You draw what you want. I'll draw what we need for Gene's college—for Dixieland, and for anything else we need.


GANT

(*Rises, crosses to office*)

I think I'll wait to cash it until I get to Chapel Hill. The bank has a branch there, doesn't it, Will?

(*Gives* WILL *his pen*)

ELIZA

Why would you want to cash it in Chapel Hill?

GANT

This is my check, isn't it? I'm the one who had the foresight to buy this little pie-cornered lot thirty-one years ago for four hundred dollars. . . . . money from the estate of Cynthia L. Gant, deceased. I guess I'm entitled to the profit.

ELIZA

Now, Mr. Gant, if you're thinking to get my dander up . . .

GANT

(*Picks up hat, puts it on*)

Miss Eliza, I've been wanting to get away from here for a long time. I'm taking Gene with me.

(*Crosses to* EUGENE)

I'm going to put him in that college there at Chapel Hill.

EUGENE

Now?

GANT

Now! And then I'm going to travel. . . . . and when Gene's free in the summer, we'll travel together.

(*Crosses back to* ELIZA)

And there's nothing in this whole wide world that you're going to do to stop me. And I can just see the word Dixieland forming on your cursed lips. What about Dixieland? Nothing for Dixieland? *No, not one God Damn red cent!* You've plenty of property of your own you can sell. If it's rest and comfort you really want, sell it, woman, sell it! But I think you like working hard, because then that makes us all feel sorry for you. And I do feel sorry for you too, from the bottom of my heart.

(*Puts check in pocket*)

Well, Eugene?

EUGENE
Papa, I can't go now.

GANT
Why not? You haven't got any better clothes . . . . so you might as well go as you are. I guess we'll say our goodbyes.

(*Addresses the angel*)

So long, dear Carrara angel. I'll arrange for us to be together again some day. (*Shakes hands with* BEN) Goodbye, Ben— Tell Helen— tell Helen I'll write to her.

ELIZA
(*Leaping at* GANT)

I won't let you do this. I won't let you.

EUGENE
*Mama!*

ELIZA
(*Seizes check from* GANT's *pocket, tears it up, flings it on the ground*)

All right, all right, all right! There's your check. I guess there's nothing to prevent you from going to the bank and trying to get another check, but it won't work because I'm going to put an injunction against you. I'll prove you're not responsible to sell this property, or even to own it. I'll get guardianship over you! Everyone knows

the times you've been to the cure—the threats you've made to me.
. . . the times you've tried to kill me—I'll tell them. You're a madman, Mr. Gant, a madman. You're not going to get away with this.
I'll fight you tooth and nail, tooth and nail. And I'll win.

(*Trembling, she picks up her handbag from the stone seat.*)

GANT

All the things you've said about me are true, Eliza. I've only brought
you pain. Why don't you let me go?

ELIZA

Because you're my husband, Mr. Gant! You're my husband. Thirty-
one years together and we'll go on—we must go on. A house divided against itself cannot stand. We must try to understand and
love each other. We must try. . . .

(ELIZA *exits.*)

GANT

(*Quietly*)

Take her home, will you, Will?

(WILL *hurries after* ELIZA. *A long moment.* BEN, *weak and feverish, dries his forehead with his handkerchief.* GANT *sinks into a
chair.*)

GANT

Eugene, go over to Laughran's and get me a bottle. You heard me.

EUGENE

No, Papa.

GANT

Are you still padding along after your mother?

BEN

Leave Gene alone. If you want to get sick, do it yourself.

GANT

Ungrateful sons! Oh, the sad waste of years, the red wound of all our mistakes.

(GANT *rises, exits.* EUGENE *looks after his father.*)

BEN

The fallen Titan. He might have succeeded if he hadn't tried to take you. He could still make it, but he won't try again.

EUGENE

They loved each other once. They must have had one moment in time that was perfect. What happened? It frightens me, Ben. How can something so perfect turn into this torture?

BEN

They're strangers. They don't know each other. No one ever really comes to know anyone.

EUGENE

That's not true. I know you—I know Laura.

BEN

Listen to him! No matter what arms may clasp us, what heart may warm us, what mouth may kiss us, we remain strangers. We never escape it. Never, never, never.

(*Closes eyes, leans back*)

EUGENE

Ben! Hey, Ben?

(*Worriedly crosses down to* BEN, *feels his face*)

Ben, you're burning up! Come on . . .

(*Tries to lift him*)

Put your arms around me. I'm going to take you home.


BEN

(*Sinks back*)

Can't. It's all right, I'm just tired.


EUGENE

Why didn't you tell somebody you're sick, you crazy idiot!

(EUGENE *again tries to lift* BEN.)


BEN

To hell with them, Gene. To hell with them all. Don't give a damn for anything. Nothing gives a damn for you. There are a lot of bad days, there are a lot of good ones—

(EUGENE *rushes into the office, picks up the telephone.*)

that's all there is . . . . a lot of days. . . . My God, is there no freedom on this earth?


EUGENE

(*Into telephone*)

Get me Dr. Maguire quickly. *It's my brother Ben!*


BEN

(*Stirs, in anguish, looks up at the Carrara angel*)

And still you smile. . . . .


CURTAIN

# ACT TWO

*Scene 2*

*It is the next night; a painful tenseness grips the house.*

LAURA *and* EUGENE *sit together on the yard seat.* MRS. PERT *sits motionless in her rocker near the front door.* HUGH *slowly walks about. The inside hall is lighted, as is* BEN'S *room, which we see for the first time. There* DR. MAGUIRE *and* HELEN *are hovering over* BEN'S *still body.* GANT *is at the hall telephone.*

GANT

(*Shouting into telephone*)

Second class seaman, Luke Gant. G-A-N-T—Gant!

(*Angrily*)

I don't know why you can't hear me.

HUGH

(*Crosses to door*)

W.O., you don't have to shout because it's long distance.

GANT

Shut up, Hugh, I know what I'm doing.

(*Into telephone*)

Do what? I am standing back from the telephone. All right, all right. . . .

(*Moves telephone away from him, lower*)

Can you hear me now? Of all the perversities. Very well, I will repeat. Yesterday I sent a telegram to my son, Luke Gant, to come home, that his brother Ben has pneumonia. Can you tell me if—oh, he did leave? Why didn't he let us know? All right! Thank you. Thank you very much.

(*Hangs up, joins the others on the veranda*)

HUGH
They gave him leave?

GANT
If he made good connections he ought to be here by now.

HUGH
Ben'll be all right, W.O.

GANT
I remember when little Grover was ill in St. Louis, and Eliza sent for me. I didn't get there on time.

(*Sits on yard stool.* ELIZA *enters from the house.*)

ELIZA
Did you reach him?

GANT
He's on his way.

ELIZA
It's all nonsense, of course. Ben is far from dying. But you do like to dramatize, Mr. Gant. Still, it will be good to see Luke. . . .

EUGENE
(*Crosses to* ELIZA)
Mama, when can I see Ben?

ELIZA

When the doctor says. I'll tell you what: when you go in there, don't make out like Ben is sick. Just make a big joke of it—laugh as big as you please—

EUGENE

(Groans)

Mama!

ELIZA

Well, it's the sick one's frame of mind that counts. I remember when I was teaching school in Hominy township, I had pneumonia. Nobody expected me to live, but I did . . . I got through it somehow. I remember one day I was sitting down—I reckon I was convalescing, as the fella says. Old Doc Fletcher had been there—and as he left I saw him shake his head at my cousin Sally. "Why, Eliza, what on earth," she says, just as soon as he had gone, "he tells me you're spitting up blood every time you cough; you've got consumption as sure as you live!" "Pshaw!" I said. I remember I was just determined to make a big joke of it. "I don't believe a word of it," I said. "Not one single word." And it was because I didn't believe it that *I got well.*

GANT

(Quietly)

Eliza, don't run on so.

HELEN

(Appears on veranda)

The doctor says Mama can come in for a few minutes, but no one else yet.

EUGENE

How is he?

HELEN
You know Dr. Maguire. If you can get anything out of him. . . .

(ELIZA *takes a big breath; she and* HELEN *go into house.*)

GANT
Oh God, I don't like the feel of it. I don't like the feel of it.

BEN
(*Weakly*)
Maguire, if you don't stop hanging over me I'll smother to death.

MAGUIRE
(*To* ELIZA *and* HELEN *as they enter*)
With both of you in here soaking up oxygen, leave that door open.

(ELIZA *advances slowly to* BEN, *swallows a gasp at the sight of the tortured, wasted body.* BEN's *eyes are closed.*)

HELEN
Mama's here, Ben.

ELIZA
(*Speaking as though to a baby*)
Why hello, son—did you think I wasn't ever coming in to see you?

HELEN
(*After a pause*)
Ben, Mama's here.

ELIZA

(*To* MAGUIRE)

Can't he talk? Why doesn't he look at me?

MAGUIRE

Ben, you can hear what's going on, can't you?

BEN

(*Quietly, his eyes still closed*)

I wish you'd all get out and leave me alone.

ELIZA

What kind of talk is that? You have to be looked after, son!

BEN

Then let Mrs. Pert look after me.

HELEN

Ben!

BEN

Maguire, where's Fatty? I want to see Fatty.

HELEN

Ben, how can you talk that way? Your mother and your sister? If it weren't for that woman you wouldn't be sick now. Drinking, carousing with her night after night—

BEN

(*Yells with dwindling strength*)

Fatty! Fatty!

(*On the veranda,* MRS. PERT *stands quickly, then enters house.*)

HELEN

(*To* BEN)

You ought to be ashamed of yourself!

DR. MAGUIRE

Mrs. Gant, we need some more cold cloths. Why don't you . . .

HELEN

(*Angrily to* MAGUIRE)

Fiend! Do you have to add to her misery? When you need something, ask me.

(ELIZA, *starting out of* BEN'S *room, meets* MRS. PERT *in doorway.* MRS. PERT *hesitates.*)

DR. MAGUIRE

That's all right, Mrs. Pert.

BEN

(*Immediately turns toward her*)

Fatty?

DR. MAGUIRE

Ben seems to want you here, that's all I care about.

(*To* HELEN)

You'll be called if you're needed.

HELEN

This is the last time you come into this house, Dr. Maguire!

(HELEN *leaves the room. Outside* BEN'S *door* ELIZA *hands some cold cloths to* HELEN. HELEN *reenters* BEN'S *room, places them on the bureau.*)

BEN

Fatty, stay by me. Sing to me. "A Baby's Prayer at Twilight" . . .

FATTY

(*Sitting beside him*)

Sh-h-h, Ben. Be quiet, dear. Save yourself.

BEN

Hold my hand, Fatty.

FATTY

(*Takes his hand, sings*)

"Just a baby's prayer at twilight
When lights are low
A baby's years
Are filled with tears
Hmmmm hmmmm hmmmm."

(*Hearing the voice,* EUGENE *stands, looks up toward* BEN'S *room.* HELEN *and* ELIZA *appear on the veranda,* HELEN *comforting her mother.*)

EUGENE

How does he seem, Mama?

ELIZA

He couldn't stand to see me worrying. That's what it was, you know. He couldn't stand to see me worrying about him.

GANT

(*Groaning*)

Oh Jesus, it's fearful—that this should be put on me, old and sick as I am—

HELEN

(*In blazing fury*)

You shut your mouth this minute, you damned old man. I've spent my life taking care of you! Everything's been done for you—everything—and you'll be here when we're all gone . . . so don't let us hear anything about your sickness, you selfish old man—it makes me furious!

DR. MAGUIRE

(*Appearing on veranda*)

If any of you are interested, Ben is a little better.

EUGENE

Thank God!

HELEN

Ben is better? Why didn't you say so before?

ELIZA

I could have told you! I could have told you! I had a feeling all along!

DR. MAGUIRE

(*Crosses down steps*)

I'll be back in a little while.

GANT

Well! We can all relax now.

DR. MAGUIRE

(*Motions* EUGENE *away from the others*)

Eugene, it's both lungs now. I can't tell them. But see to it that they stay around. I'm going next door and phone for some oxygen. It may ease it a little for him. It won't be long.

(*He gives* EUGENE *a fond, strengthening touch, exits.*)

GANT

What about Luke? Luke'll be furious when he finds out he came all this way for nothing!

ELIZA

For nothing? You call Ben's getting well "for nothing"?

GANT

Oh, you know what I mean, Miss Eliza. I'm going to take a little nap.

ELIZA

You're going to take a little nip, that's what you mean.

GANT

You can come up and search my room if you don't believe me.

(*Exits into house.* EUGENE *stands, dazed and miserable. He forces himself during the following scene.* JAKE *and* FLORRY *enter from rear veranda.*)

ELIZA

(*Excitedly*)

Mr. Clatt, Miss Mangle—did you hear? Ben is getting better! The crisis is past!

JAKE

We're so happy for you, Mrs. Gant.

ELIZA

I knew all along—something told me. Oh, not that he didn't have a very high fever—I admit that—but my second sense . . .

LUKE

(Off)

Hello—o—o there!

ELIZA

(Peering off)

Luke!

(Rushes down steps)

Luke! Luke Gant!

(The boarders melt into the background as LUKE GANT, wearing a Navy uniform, carrying a lightly packed duffle bag, enters. He is attractive, slight, lighted by an enormous love of humor and life, and adored by everyone. He is the son who got away early, but he still carries the marks of a distressing childhood; he stutters sometimes.)

LUKE

Mama, Mama!

(Swings her around)

HUGH

Well, if it isn't the sailor himself! How are you?

LUKE

(Shaking hands with HUGH)

I'm fine, Hugh! How goes it?

ELIZA

Aren't you going to kiss your old mother?

**LUKE**

Old? You're getting younger and stronger by the minute.

(*Kisses her*)

**ELIZA**

I am, I am, son. I feel it—now that Ben's going to get well.

**LUKE**

The old boy is better?

**HELEN**

Luke!

**LUKE**

Helen!

**HELEN**

(*Leaps into his arms*)

How's my boy?

**LUKE**

S-s-slick as a puppy's belly. I thought you all might need cheering up. I brought you some ice cream from Woodruff's!

(*Gives carton of ice cream to* HELEN)

**HELEN**

Naturally, you wouldn't be Luke Gant if you didn't!

**EUGENE**

(*Crosses to* LUKE)

Welcome home, Luke!

**LUKE**

(*They shake hands.*)

My God, doesn't anybody buy you any clothes—and look at that hair. Mama, he looks like an orphan! Cut off those damn big feet of his, he'd go up in the air!

**EUGENE**

How long have you got, Luke?

**LUKE**

Can you s-s-stand me for twenty-four hours?

(*Sees* LAURA)

Who's this?

**ELIZA**

That's Miss James from Virginia. Laura, this is another of my sons, Luke Gant.

**LAURA**

(*Shaking hands*)

How do you do, Mr. Gant?

**LUKE**

How do you do?

**ELIZA**

(*Drawing* LUKE *away*)

All right, just come along here, and behave yourself.

**HELEN**

I'd better dish up the ice cream before it melts.

(*Exits into house*)

LUKE

(*Calling after* HELEN)

Maybe Ben would like some. I got pistachio especially for him.

ELIZA

Tell your father the admiral is here!

LUKE

Can I see Ben, now?

ELIZA

Well, the truth is, that Mrs. Pert is in there with him now.

LUKE

Mrs. Pert is?

(*Looks at the others*)

HUGH

I wouldn't go into it, Luke. It's a somewhat "fraught" subject.

LUKE

Oh boy, oh boy, I know what that is! Still the same old happy household?

(LUKE *and* ELIZA *sit on the veranda edge.*)

ELIZA

Nonsense. I have nothing against the woman except she's getting too many ideas that she's a fixture here. First thing in the morning I'm going to ask her to move.

LUKE

Doesn't she pay her rent?

ELIZA
Oh, she pays it.

LUKE
(*Laughs*)

Then you're never going to ask her to move—don't kid me! The
paying customers are what count around here! Aren't they, Mama?

ELIZA
Luke Gant, there are certain standards I have to keep up, for the
reputation of Dixieland!

LUKE
(*Never unkindly*)

What kind of standards? The old dope fiend who hung himself in
the same bedroom where Ben had to sleep for eight years after he
cut him down? And all those amateur femme fatales who bask under
your protection here, waylaying us in the hall, the bathroom—
Mama, we never had a s-s-safe moment! And people think you find
out about life in the Navy!

ELIZA
(*Playfully*)

I'm warning you, Luke! It's a good thing I know you're teasing.

(HELEN *enters with plates, dishes up ice cream.*)

LUKE
Remember the early morning when Ben and Gene and I used to
take the paper route together, remember, Gene? Old Ben used to
make up stories for us about all the sleeping people in all the sleeping houses! He always used to throw the papers as lightly as he could
because he hated to wake them. Remember, Gene?

HELEN

And that book of baseball stories Ben used to read to us by the hour—what was it, Gene?

EUGENE
(*In tears*)
*You know me, Al,* by Ring Lardner.

ELIZA
(*Leaping to* EUGENE)
Eugene. Child, what is it? What is it!

(MRS. PERT *enters hurriedly.*)

MRS. PERT
Mrs. Gant! Mrs. Gant!

HELEN
What is it, Mrs. Pert?

MRS. PERT
He can't get his breath!

HUGH
Gene, get the doctor!

(HELEN *and* ELIZA *follow* MRS. PERT *into the house.*)

ELIZA
You ridiculous woman! The doctor said he was better.

(EUGENE *exits to get* MAGUIRE. GANT *enters through side door.*)

GANT

What the hell's all the commotion about?

(*Sees* LUKE)

Luke! Welcome home!


LUKE

(*As they shake hands*)

Papa—Ben's not doing so well.


GANT

Jesus, have mercy! That I should have to bear this in my old age. Not another one—first Grover, now Ben . . .


LUKE

For God's sake, Papa, try to behave decently, for Ben's sake!

(EUGENE *and* DOC MAGUIRE *enter hurriedly.*)


GANT

(*Seizing the doctor*)

Maguire, you got to save him—you got to save him.

(MAGUIRE *pushes past* GANT *into the house, enters* BEN'S *room where the three women are gathered,* MRS. PERT *standing nearest* BEN *at the head of the bed.*)


MAGUIRE

You women step back, give him air.

(*Bends over* BEN)

GANT

(*Collapsing onto the steps*)

When the old die, no one cares. But the young . . . the young . . .

EUGENE

(*Sits beside him*)

I would care, Papa.

BEN

It's one way—to step out of—the photograph—isn't it, Fatty?

FATTY

Hush, Ben, don't say that!

HELEN

(*To the doctor*)

There must be something you can do!

MAGUIRE

(*Straightens up*)

Not all the king's horses, not all the doctors in the world can help him now.

HELEN

Have you tried everything? Everything?

MAGUIRE

My dear girl! He's drowning! Drowning!

ELIZA

(*In deep pain*)

Mrs. Pert, you're standing in my place . . .

(MRS. PERT *moves away.* ELIZA *steps close to* BEN, *sits.*)

ELIZA

Ben—son.

(*She reaches to touch him. His head turns toward her, drops. There is a last rattling, drowning sound.* BEN *dies.* MAGUIRE *checks his heart.*)

MAGUIRE

It's over. It's all over.

(HELEN, *racked, exits toward the veranda.* MRS. PERT *puts the socks she has been knitting at* BEN's *feet and exits upstairs.* HELEN *enters the veranda, tries to stifle her sobs.*)

HELEN

He's gone. Ben's gone.

(HELEN *falls into* EUGENE's *arms.* MAGUIRE, *carrying his doctor's bag, appears in the hall, puts a match to his chewed cigar.*)

EUGENE

(*Crossing up to* DOCTOR)

Did he say anything? Did he say anything at the end?

MAGUIRE

What were you expecting him to say?

EUGENE

I don't know. I just wondered.

MAGUIRE

If he found what he was looking for? I doubt that, Gene. At least
he didn't say anything.

(EUGENE *leaves and goes into* BEN'S *room.* MAGUIRE *comes out
onto the veranda.*)

LUKE

How long have you known, Doc?

MAGUIRE

For two days—from the beginning. Since I first saw him at three in
the morning in the Uneeda Lunch with a cup of coffee in one hand
and a cigarette in the other.

GANT

Was there nothing to be done?

MAGUIRE

My dear, dear Gant, we can't turn back the days that have gone. We
can't turn back to the hours when our lungs were sound, our blood
hot, our bodies young. We are a flash of fire—a brain, a heart, a
spirit. And we are three cents worth of lime and iron—which we cannot get back.

(*He shakes his head.*)

We can believe in the nothingness of life. We can believe in the
nothingness of death, and of a life after death. But who can believe
in the nothingness of Ben?

HELEN

Come on, Papa, there's nothing more to sit up for. Let me put you
to bed. Come along.

(*She takes the old man and leads him gently into the house, as
the* DOCTOR *exits.* HUGH *and* LUKE *exit after* HELEN *and* GANT. *Only*

LAURA *is left, still sitting on the yard seat.* EUGENE, *who has been standing in the corner in* BEN's *room, goes to his mother, who is holding* BEN's *hand tightly.*)

EUGENE

Mama?

ELIZA

He doesn't turn away from me any more.

EUGENE

(*Takes her hand, tries gently to disengage* BEN's)

Mama, you've got to let go. You've got to let go, Mama!

(ELIZA *shakes her head, her rough clasp tightening.* EUGENE *leaves the room, comes out to the veranda. There, slowly, he sinks to his knees, prays.* LAURA *watches him, her heart going out to him.*)

EUGENE

Whoever You are, be good to Ben tonight. Whoever You are, be good to Ben tonight . . . Whoever You are . . . be good to Ben tonight. . . . be good to Ben tonight. . . . .

*SLOW   CURTAIN*

ACT THREE

# ACT THREE

THE DIXIELAND BOARDING HOUSE

*Two weeks later.*

*The house is seen in a soft early light. From offstage, a newsboy, whistling, throws four tightly wadded newspapers onto the veranda—plop—plop—plop—plop. The whistling and his steps fade away. The lights come up dimly in* LAURA's *room.* LAURA *is in bed in her nightgown.* EUGENE *is at the foot of the bed by the window, looking out. He takes his shirt from the bedpost, puts it on.*

LAURA
*(Stirring)*

Gene? What was that?

EUGENE

Soaks Baker with the morning papers. Plop—plop—plop—plop—how I used to love that sound. Every time the heavy bag getting lighter. I'll always feel sorry for people who have to carry things.

*(Sighs)*

It's getting light, it's nearly dawn.

LAURA
Don't go yet.

*(Reaches for his hand)*

EUGENE
Do you think I want to on your last morning here? Mama gets up

so early. Do you know that every morning before she cooks breakfast she visits Ben's grave?

(*Sits on bed, takes her in his arms*)

LAURA

Gene, Gene.

EUGENE

Oh, Laura, I love you so. When I'm close to you like this, it's so
natural. Are all men like me? Tell me.

LAURA

I've told you I've never known anyone like you.

EUGENE

But you have known men? It would be strange if you hadn't. A
woman so beautiful, so loving. You make me feel like I only used
to dream of feeling. I've hardly thought to daydream in weeks—
except about us.

LAURA

What did you used to dream?

EUGENE

I always wanted to be the winner, the general, the spearhead of
victory! Then, following that, I wanted to be loved. Victory and love!
Unbeaten and beloved. And I am that now, truly! Laura, will you
marry me?

LAURA

(*Moving away*)

Oh darling!

EUGENE

You knew I was going to ask you, didn't you? You knew I couldn't let you go even for a day.

LAURA

Yes, I knew.

EUGENE

You're happy with me. You know I make you happy. And I'm so complete with you.

(*He draws her back into his arms.*)

Do you know that three hundred dollars Ben left me? He would want me to use it for us. I'll go with you to Richmond today. I'll meet your parents, so they won't think I'm an irresponsible fool who's stolen you. That may be a little hard to prove—but there is a job I can get. Would you mind living in Altamont?

LAURA

I don't care where I live. Just keep holding me.

EUGENE

I am going to have to tell Mama first.

LAURA

Let's not worry about that now. Tell me about us.

EUGENE

All the treasures the world has in store for us? We'll see and know them all . . . All the things and the places I've read about. There isn't a state in this country we won't know. The great names of Arizona, Texas, Colorado, California—we'll ride the freights to get there if we have to. And we'll go to Europe, and beyond . . . the cool, green land of Shakespeare, the gloomy forests of Gaul, the great Assyrian plains where Alexander feasted . . . the crumbling walls of Babylon, the palaces of the kings of Egypt, the towering white crags of Switzerland . . . My God, Laura, there might not be time enough for all!

LAURA

There will be time enough, darling.

(*They kiss longingly. From a far distance, they hear the whistle of a train as it passes.*)

EUGENE

The Richmond train leaves at noon. I'll have to get packed.

LAURA

You do love trains, don't you?

EUGENE

I love only you. Will you have confidence in me, the unbeaten and beloved?

LAURA

Yes, darling, I will have confidence in you.

EUGENE

I'll never have to sneak out of this room again.

(EUGENE *rises, moves to the door.* LAURA, *on her knees, reaches toward him.*)

LAURA

Eugene!

(*He comes back to her.*)

I will love you always.

(*They kiss.* EUGENE *exits.* LAURA *leaps from the bed, hurries after him.*)

LAURA

Gene!

(ELIZA *has come out the side door. She takes flowers out of a bucket preparing to take them to* BEN's *grave.* EUGENE *enters the hallway, lifts the phone receiver. He doesn't see* ELIZA. *Lights dim down on* LAURA's *room as she dresses.*)

EUGENE

(*Into telephone*)

Good morning. 3-2 please. Hello, Uncle Will? This is Eugene. Yes, I know how early it is . . . You know that position you offered me? I've decided to take it.

ELIZA

(*Pleased, to herself*)

Well, can you imagine!

EUGENE

(*Into telephone*)

I've thought it over, and that's what I'd like to do, for a while anyway. That's right. That's fine . . . Well, you see, I'm getting married . . .

(ELIZA *freezes in pain.*)

Yes, married—to Miss James. We're going to Richmond for a few days. We're leaving on the noon train. Thanks, Uncle Will. Thanks a lot.

(EUGENE *hangs up. He starts to go back upstairs.*)

ELIZA

Eugene!


EUGENE

(*Coming out to her slowly*)

Well, now—with your second sense, I thought you would have guessed it, Mama.


ELIZA

First Grover, then Ben, now you . . . Why didn't I know, why didn't I see?


EUGENE

I'm sorry, Mama, but we couldn't wait any longer.


ELIZA

Gene, child, don't make this mistake. She's so much older than you. Don't throw yourself away, boy!


EUGENE

Mama, there's no use arguing. Nothing you can say will change my mind.


ELIZA

(*Desperately*)

And my plans for you? What of my plans for you?


EUGENE

Mama, I don't want your plans, I've got my own life to live!


ELIZA

But you don't know! Gene, listen, you know that Stumptown property of mine? I sold it just yesterday so you could go to Chapel Hill

—You know I've always wanted you to have an education. You can have it now, child, you can have it.

EUGENE

It's too late, Mama, it's too late!

ELIZA

Why law, child, it's never too late for anything! It's what Ben wanted, you know.

EUGENE

Laura and I are leaving, Mama. I'm going up to get packed.

(*He briefly kisses her, exits into house.*)

ELIZA

Gene!

(ELIZA *stands looking after him a moment, then quickly enters the hall, lifts the telephone receiver.*)

Three-two, please.

(HELEN *enters from the kitchen with a broom. She sweeps the veranda.*)

HELEN

What are you calling Uncle Will so early for?

ELIZA

(*Into phone*)

Will? No, no, I know—I heard . . . Yes, I know it's early . . . Listen, Will, I want you to do something for me. You know my Stumptown property? I want you to sell it . . . Now, this morning. Will, don't argue with me—I don't care what it's worth. Call Cash Rankin, he's been after me for weeks to sell . . . Well, I know what

I want to do—I'll explain it to you later— Just do what I say and let me know.

(*She hangs up.*)

HELEN
Well, it's never too early in the morning to turn a trade, is it? What are you selling?

ELIZA
Some property I own.

HELEN
Maybe you can put a little of that money into getting somebody else to help you at that altar of yours, the kitchen stove.

ELIZA
Helen, get breakfast started, will you? I'll be in later. And if Gene comes down, keep him in there, will you?

HELEN
Oh, all right. You let me know when I can let him out!

(*Exits into house.* ELIZA *appears at door of* LAURA'S *room.* LAURA *is dressed and is packing her suitcase.* ELIZA *knocks.*)

LAURA
(*As* ELIZA *enters*)
Oh, Mrs. Gant. I've been expecting you. Come in.

ELIZA
I should think you would.

LAURA
Mrs. Gant, before you say anything . . .

ELIZA

I'll vow, I can't believe a mature woman—at a time of trouble like this—would take advantage of a child, a mere child . . .

LAURA

Mrs. Gant, will you please listen.

ELIZA

I will listen to nothing. You just pack your things and get out of this house. I should have known what you were from the first minute I set eyes on you . . . "I'm looking for a room, Mrs. Gant . . ." Why, butter wouldn't melt in your mouth . . .

LAURA

(*Slowly, distinctly*)

Mrs. Gant, I am not marrying Eugene. I'm not. I wish with all my heart I could.

ELIZA

You can't lie out of it. Gene just told me.

LAURA

I am engaged to be married to a young man in Richmond.

ELIZA

What kind of a wicked game are you playing with my child?

LAURA

Mrs. Gant, this isn't easy. I should have told Gene long ago . . . but I didn't. A girl about to get married suddenly finds herself facing responsibilities. I never liked responsibilities. Gene knows how I am. I like music, I like to walk in the woods, I like . . . to dream. I know I'm older than Gene, but in many ways I'm younger. The thought of marriage frightened me. I told my fiancé I needed time to think it over. I fell in love with Eugene. I found the kind of romance I'd never known before, but I've also found that it isn't the answer. Gene is a wonderful boy, Mrs. Gant. He must go to college. He must have room to expand and grow, to find himself. He mustn't be tied down at this point in his life. He needs the whole world to wander in—and I know now that I need a home, I need children— I need a husband. For people like me there are rules, very good rules for marriage and for happiness—and I've broken enough of them. I telephoned Philip last night. He's arriving at the depot on that early train. We're going on to Charleston together, and we'll be married there. He loves me, and I will love him too after a while.

(*Takes note from desk*)

I left this note for Eugene. I couldn't just tell him.

(*Gives it to* ELIZA)

Will you say goodbye to Mr. Gant for me, and tell him I hope he feels better? And my goodbyes to Mr. Clatt and the others? And to Helen. Especially to Helen. She works so hard.

(*Looks around*)

Goodbye, little room. I've been happy here.

(*Picks up suitcase, faces* ELIZA)

Some day you're going to have to let him go, too. Goodbye, Mrs. Gant.

(*She exits. During the above* HUGH *has entered the veranda, is seated, reading the newspaper.* LAURA *enters from the house, looks back lingeringly, then, hearing the approaching train, hurries off toward the station.* HELEN *enters, drinking coffee.*)

HELEN
Mama? Now where on earth. Hugh, have you seen Mama?

HUGH
Umph.

HELEN

Do you know she was on the phone just now selling some property? Imagine—at this hour! And she leaves me to slave in the kitchen . . . Do you know where she is?

HUGH

You know, they don't advertise the good jobs in here, not the really big ones.

GANT

(*Entering in his suspenders, sleepily rubbing his jaw*)

Isn't breakfast ready yet?

HELEN

Papa, how many times has Mama told you, you wait until the boarders have had theirs! And don't you dare appear in front of them in your suspenders, do you hear?

GANT

Merciful God! What a way to greet the day!

(*He exits.*)

HELEN

(*Calling after* GANT)

Papa, do you know where Mama is?

(HELEN *exits after* GANT. EUGENE *enters down stairs, carrying his suitcase, stops at* LAURA's *door, knocks.* ELIZA *has just laid* LAURA's *letter on the bed.*)

EUGENE

Laura? Laura?

(EUGENE *enters to* ELIZA.)

Mama! Where's Laura? Where is she?

ELIZA

She's gone.

EUGENE

Gone? Where?

ELIZA

She just walked out on you, child. Just walked out on you.

(*Shakes her finger at him*)

I could have told you, the minute I laid eyes on her—

EUGENE

(*Seizing* ELIZA's *hand*)

You sent her away.

ELIZA

I never did. She just walked out on you, child.

(EUGENE *breaks for the door.* ELIZA *picks up the letter, runs after him.*)

ELIZA

Gene! Eugene! Wait!

EUGENE

(*Runs down to the veranda*)

Laura . . .

(*Looks up street*)

Laura . . .

(As HUGH *points toward station, starts off that way*)

Laura . . .

ELIZA
(*Entering, waving the letter*)
Wait! Wait! She left you this. Gene!

(EUGENE *turns, sees the letter.*)

She left you this. Read it, child.

(EUGENE *crosses to* ELIZA, *takes the letter, tears it open, reads it.*)

ELIZA
You see, it's no use. It's no use.

(EUGENE *crosses slowly to the yard seat, sits.* ELIZA *watches him.* HELEN *enters through the front door.*)

HELEN
Mama, there you are! Where have you been? We've got to start getting breakfast.

(As ELIZA *waves her to silence*)

What's the matter?

ELIZA
That Miss James. She and Eugene . . .

HELEN
(*Laughs*)
Oh my God, Mama, have you just found out about that? What about it?

ELIZA
She's gone.

HELEN

What?

ELIZA

She just walked out on him.

HELEN

(*Crosses to* EUGENE)

Oh ho, so that's it, is it? Has your girl gone and left you, huh? Huh?

(*Tickles his ribs. He turns, clasps her knees.*)

Why, Gene, forget about it! You're only a kid yet. She's a grown woman.

ELIZA

Helen's right. Why, child, I wouldn't let a girl get the best of me. She was just fooling you all the time, just leading you on, wasn't she, Helen?

HELEN

You'll forget her in a week, Gene.

ELIZA

Why, of course you will. Pshaw, this was just puppy love. Like the fellow says, there's plenty good fish in the sea as ever came out of it.

HELEN

Cheer up, you're not the only man got fooled in his life!

HUGH

(*From behind his paper*)

By God, that's the truth!

(HELEN *and* ELIZA *glare at* HUGH.)

ELIZA

Helen, go inside, I'll be in in a minute.

HELEN

Oh, all right. Hugh, you come in and help me.

(HELEN *exits, followed by* HUGH.)

ELIZA
(*Sits beside* EUGENE, *his back still turned to her*)

Gene. You know what I'd do if I were you? I'd just show her I was a good sport, that's what! I wouldn't let on to her that it affected me one bit. I'd write her just as big as you please and laugh about the whole thing.

EUGENE

Oh, God, Mama, please, leave me alone, leave me alone!

ELIZA

Why, I'd be ashamed to let any girl get my goat like that. When you get older, you'll just look back on this and laugh. You'll see. You'll be going to college next year, and you won't remember a thing about it.

(EUGENE *turns, looks at her.*)

I told you I'd sold that Stumptown property, and I have. This year's term has started already but next year . . .

EUGENE

Mama, *now! Now!* I've wasted enough time!

ELIZA

What are you talking about? Why you're a child yet, there's plenty of time yet . . .

EUGENE

*(Rises, walks about her)*

Mama, Mama, what is it? What more do you want from me? Do you want to strangle and drown me completely? Do you want more string? Do you want me to collect more bottles? Tell me what you want! Do you want more property? Do you want the town? Is that it?

ELIZA

Why, I don't know what you're talking about, boy. If I hadn't tried to accumulate a little something, none of you would have had a roof to call your own.

EUGENE

A roof to call our own? Good God, I never had a bed to call my own! I never had a room to call my own! I never had a quilt to call my own that wasn't taken from me to warm the mob that rocks on that porch and grumbles.

ELIZA

*(Rises, looking for an escape)*

Now you may sneer at the boarders if you like . . .

EUGENE

No, I can't. There's not breath or strength enough in me to sneer at them all I like. Ever since I was this high, and you sent me to the store for the groceries, I used to think, this food is not for us—it's for them! Mama, making us wait until they've eaten, all these years —feeding us on *their* leftovers—do you know what it does to us— when it's you we wanted for us, *you* we needed for us. Why? Why?

ELIZA

(*Trembling*)

They don't hurt me like the rest of you do—they wouldn't talk to me like you are, for one thing.

(*Starts toward side door*)

EUGENE

Because they don't care—they're strangers. They don't give a damn about you! They'll talk like this about you behind your back—I've heard them do that plenty!

ELIZA

(*Turns*)

What? What? What kind of things do they say about me?

EUGENE

What does it matter what they say—*they* say! Doesn't it matter to you what I say?

(*Takes her in his arms, holds her*)

ELIZA

(*Beginning to weep*)

I don't understand.

EUGENE

(*Releases her, moves away*)

Oh it's easy to cry now, Mama, but it won't do you any good! I've done as much work for my wages as you deserve. I've given you fair value for your money, I thank you for nothing.

(*Crosses up to veranda*)

ELIZA

What's that? What are you saying!

EUGENE

I said I thank you for nothing, but I take that back. Yes, I have a great deal to be thankful for. I give thanks for every hour of loneliness I've had here, for every dirty cell you ever gave me to sleep in, for the ten million hours of indifference, and for these two minutes of cheap advice.

ELIZA

You will be punished if there's a just God in Heaven.

EUGENE

Oh, there is! I'm sure there is! Because I have been punished. By God, I shall spend the rest of my life getting my heart back, healing and forgetting every scar you put upon me when I was a child. The first move I ever made after the cradle was to crawl for the door. And every move I ever made since has been an effort to escape. And now, at last I am free from all of you. And I shall get me some order out of this chaos. I shall find my way out of it yet, though it takes me twenty years more—alone.

ELIZA

Gene! Gene, you're not leaving?

EUGENE

Ah, you were not looking, were you? I've already gone.

(EUGENE *exits into the house, into* LAURA's *room, where he left his valise. He throws his body on the bed, stifles his crying.* ELIZA *sits on the veranda edge, stunned.* GANT, *wearing a vest over his suspenders, enters.*)

GANT

Now do you suppose I can get some breakfast?

(ELIZA *doesn't answer.*)

Well, do you mind if I make a fire in the fireplace?

(*Goes to wood box, muttering*)

If I can't get any food to keep me alive, I can get a little warmth out of this drafty barn!

(*Starts collecting wood from box*)

Some day I'm going to burn up this house—just pile in all the logs that old grate'll hold—and all the furniture—and all the wooden-headed people around here—and some kerosene—till this old barn takes off like a giant cinder blazing through the sky. That would show them—all fifteen miserable rooms—burning, blistering . . .

ELIZA
I wish you would, Mr. Gant. I just wish you would.

GANT
You think I'm joking.

ELIZA
No, I don't.

GANT
If I just get drunk enough, I will!

ELIZA
(*Rises, faces house*)
Serve it right . . . miserable, unholy house!

GANT
Why, Miss Eliza!

ELIZA
I'll do it myself—

(*With demoniacal strength she shakes a newel post by the steps.*)

I'll tear you down! I'll kill you, house, kill you! I'll shake you to pieces!

(*Picks up* MRS. PERT'S *rocker, crashes it*)

HELEN
(*Entering hurriedly*)

Eliza Gant, have you gone mad!

GANT

Let me help you, Mrs. Gant!

(*Drops wood, starts tearing at the other post*)

God-damned barn! Thief! Travesty on nature!

ELIZA

God-damned barn!

(*Kicks in latticed panels under the veranda*)

HELEN
(*Calls inside*)

Hugh, come out here!

WILL
(*Entering from rear of veranda*)

My God, what are they doing?

GANT
(*Screaming up at house*)

Clatt—Mangle—Brown— Come out of there, you rats, all of you— come out, come out, wherever you are!

(*The boarders begin to yell and squeal from inside.*)

ELIZA

(*Hysterically, imitating* GANT)

Come out, come out, wherever you are!

HUGH

(*Entering*)

What's going on?

GANT

(*Breaking off the newel post*)

We're tearing down this murderous trap, that's what. Hand me the hatchet, Hugh. It's in the wood box.

HUGH

Fine! Fine!

(*Dashes to woodbox, takes out hatchet. The boarders enter down the stairs in various stages of undress.*)

MISS BROWN

Call the police.

MRS. CLATT

Let's get to Mrs. Haskell's!

JAKE

Gant's off his nut!

GANT

(*Chasing, threatening the boarders*)

Squeal, you croaking bastards. Croak and run! Run for your lives!

BOARDERS
(*Fleeing*)

The house is falling down!
It's a tornado!
Ladies' Temperance Society, humph!
Has anyone called the police?

HUGH
Here's the hatchet, W.O.

GANT
(*Leaping for it*)

Give it to me.

WILL
Stop it, Gant—stop this! Have you all lost your minds?

ELIZA
(*Throwing flower pot after the boarders*)

Go to Mrs. Haskell's!

HELEN
Mama!

GANT
(*Brandishing hatchet at* JAKE *and* MRS. CLATT *as they exit*)

Look at 'em run! And they haven't even had breakfast. Run, scatter-
brains, empty bellies!

JAKE
I'll sue you for this, Gant, I'll sue you for this!

(*Exits*)

(MRS. SNOWDEN *enters through front door.* GANT *whirls on her.*)

GANT

So you don't like the food here? So you don't like my wife's coffee!

(MRS. SNOWDON, *screaming, hastily retreats.*)

ELIZA

(*Lifting a chair to hurl after the boarders*)

Why, law, that's good coffee!

(HELEN *seizes* ELIZA's *arms, stops her.* ELIZA's *sensibilities slowly return.*)

GANT

Look at 'em run! Oh, Miss Eliza, what  a woman you are!

(GANT, *roaring with laughter, crosses down to* ELIZA, *is about to embrace her, sees her sober, shocked face.*)

ELIZA

Mr. Gant, Mr. Gant, what have you done? What have you done?

GANT

What have I done? What have I— Merciful God, woman!

ELIZA

Just look at this mess! And the boarders have all gone!

HELEN

I don't know what got into you, Papa.

GANT

Merciful God! What got into me? Didn't she just stand there herself and . . .

ELIZA

Helen, go get the boarders, tell them he's been drinking, tell them anything, but get them back!

WILL

I never saw such an exhibition.

ELIZA

Will, go with Helen. Tell them we all apologize. They'll listen to you. Hugh, help me clean up this mess.

(HELEN *and* WILL *exit after the boarders.*)

GANT

Let them go, Miss Eliza. *Let the boarders go!*

(ELIZA *stands rigid.* GANT *waits anxiously.*)

ELIZA

I just don't know what came over me.

GANT

(*Crosses, flings the hatchet in the woodbox*)
Merciful God!

(EUGENE *enters with his suitcase.*)

GANT

Where are you going?

EUGENE

I'm going to school at Chapel Hill, Papa.

GANT

You are?

(*He looks at* ELIZA.)

EUGENE

Mama promised me the money. She sold her Stumptown property.

GANT

Oh? By God, maybe it isn't going to be such a god-damned miserable day, after all! Got any money, son?

EUGENE

I've got Ben's money. Thanks, Papa.

GANT

(*Takes money from his pocket, tucks it into* EUGENE's *pocket*)

Well go, Gene. Go for both of us. Keep right on going.

EUGENE

I will, Papa. Goodbye.

GANT

(*As they shake hands*)

Goodbye, Gene.

(*Starts into house, turns*)

You're going to bust loose, boy—you're going to bust loose, all over this dreary planet!

(GANT *exits.* ELIZA *starts picking up the debris.*)

ELIZA

I reckon you've made up your mind all right.

EUGENE
Yes, Mama, I have.


ELIZA
Well, I'll deposit the money in the Chapel Hill Bank for you. I tell you what! It looks mighty funny, though, that you can't just stay a day or two more with Ben gone and all. It seems you'll do anything to get away from me. That's all right, I know your mind's made up and I'm not complaining! It seems all I've ever been fit for around here is to cook and sew. That's all the use any of you have ever had for me . . .


EUGENE
Mama, don't think you can work on my feelings here at the last minute.


ELIZA
It seems I've hardly laid eyes on you all summer long . . .

(*Replacing wood in woodbox*)

Well, when you get up there, you want to look up your Uncle Emerson and Aunt Lucy. Your Aunt Lucy took a great liking to you when they were down here, and when you're in a strange town it's mighty good sometimes to have someone you know. And say, when you see your Uncle Emerson, you might just tell him not to be surprised to see me any time now.

(*She nods pertly at him.*)

I reckon I can pick right up and light out the same as the next fellow when I get ready. I'm not going to spend all my days slaving away for a lot of boarders—it don't pay. If I can turn a couple of trades here this fall, I just may start out to see the world like I always intended to. I was talking to Cash Rankin the other day . . . he said, "Why Mrs. Gant," he said, "if I had your head for figures, I'd be a rich man in . . ."

*(Her talk drifts off.* EUGENE *stands looking at her. There is another terrible silence between them. She points at him with her finger, finally—her old loose masculine gesture.)*

Here's the thing I'm going to do. You know that lot of mine on Sunset Terrace, right above Dick Webster's place? Well, I been thinking. If we started to build there right away, we could be in our own house by spring. I've been thinking about it a lot lately . . .

*(There is another silence.)*

I hate to see you go, son.


EUGENE

Goodbye, Mama.


ELIZA

Try to be happy, child, try to be a little more happy . . .

*(She turns and, with unsteady step, starts into the house.)*


EUGENE

MAMA!

*(He drops the valise, takes the steps in a single bound, catching* ELIZA's *rough hands which she has held clasped across her body, drawing them to his breast.)*

GOODBYE, . . GOODBYE . . . GOODBYE . . . MAMA . . .


ELIZA

*(Holding him)*

Poor child . . . poor child . . . poor child.

*(Huskily, faintly)*

We must try to love one another.

(*Finally,* EUGENE *moves from* ELIZA, *picks up the valise as the lights start dimming, holding a spot on her.* ELIZA *seems to recede in the distance as into his memory.*)

ELIZA

Now for Heaven's sake, spruce up, boy, spruce up! Throw your shoulders back! And smile, look pleasant! Let them know up there that you *are* somebody!

(ELIZA's *voice fades. The set is black. A spot holds on* EUGENE.)

# EPILOGUE

So you're finally going, Gene?

Ben? Is that you, Ben?

Who did you think it was, you little idiot? Do you know why you're going, or are you just taking a ride on a train?

I know. Of course I know why I'm going. There's nothing here for me. Ben, what really happens? Everything is going. Everything changes and passes away. Can you remember some of the things I do? I've already forgotten the old faces. I forget the names of people I knew for years. I get their faces mixed. I get their heads stuck on other people's bodies. I think one man has said what another said. And I forget. There is something I have lost and can't remember.

The things you have forgotten and are trying to remember are the child that you were. He's gone, Gene, as I am gone. And will never return. No matter where you search for him, in a million streets, in a thousand cities.

Then I'll search for an end to hunger, and the happy land!

BEN'S VOICE

Ah, there is no happy land. There is no end to hunger!

EUGENE

Ben, help me! You must have an answer. Help me, and I won't go searching for it.

BEN'S VOICE

You little fool, what do you want to find out there?

EUGENE

*I want to find the world. Where is the world?*

BEN'S VOICE

*(Fading)*

The world is nowhere, Gene . . .

EUGENE

Ben, wait! Answer me!

BEN'S VOICE

The world is nowhere, no one, Gene. *You* are your world.

(*The train whistle sounds. Lights reveal* DIXIELAND *in dim silhouette.* EUGENE, *without looking back, exits.*)

CURTAIN